299

D0276331

Britain for Sale

Leeds City College
Withdrawn From Stock

THOMAS DANBY		
LIBRARY ✓		
CLASS NO.	338.83 BRU	
ACC. NO.	029794	

ALEX BRUMMER

Britain for Sale

British Companies in Foreign Hands
– the Hidden Threat to Our Economy

BUSINESS
BOOKS

Published by Random House Business Books 2012

2 4 6 8 10 9 7 5 3 1

Copyright © Alex Brummer 2012

Alex Brummer has asserted his right under the Copyright, Designs
and Patents Act, 1988, to be identified as the author of this work

This book is sold subject to the condition that it shall not, by way of trade or
otherwise, be lent, resold, hired out, or otherwise circulated without the
publisher's prior consent in any form of binding or cover other than that in
which it is published and without a similar condition, including this
condition, being imposed on the subsequent purchaser.

First published in Great Britain in 2012 by
Random House Business Books
Random House, 20 Vauxhall Bridge Road,
London SW1V 2SA

www.randomhouse.co.uk

Addresses for companies within The Random House Group Limited can be found at:
www.randomhouse.co.uk/offices.htm

The Random House Group Limited Reg. No. 954009

A CIP catalogue record for this book
is available from the British Library

ISBN 9781847940759

The Random House Group Limited supports The Forest Stewardship
Council (FSC®), the leading international forest certification organisation.
Our books carrying the FSC label are printed on FSC® certified paper. FSC is the
only forest certification scheme endorsed by the leading environmental organisations,
including Greenpeace. Our paper procurement policy can be found at:
www.randomhouse.co.uk/environment

Typeset by SX Composing DTP, Rayleigh, Essex
Printed and bound by CPI Group (UK) Ltd, Croydon, CR0 4YY

To Rafi, Natasha and Benjamin, a new generation

Contents

Preface

As a nation we have always been obsessed by ownership. Much of the wealth of our great families is tied up in land ownership. Huge efforts are made to ensure estates, built up over centuries and decades, are developed and preserved for the next generation. The natural inclination of those who have been successful in their careers, whether in business, politics or the professions, is to buy a country home and land. The phrase 'an Englishman's home is his castle', first coined in a seventeenth-century law book, is as relevant today as it was then.

As citizens of the United Kingdom most of us take an enormous pride in the traditions of the country in which we live. We may not, like our American cousins, plant the national flag in our gardens or wear the national emblem as lapel badges or brooches. But we relish the pageantry of public life, take enormous pride in our public buildings, are generally supportive of the monarchy and follow our national sports teams with pride and passion.

We define ourselves by our nationality. The Americans, despite their fantastic achievements, are viewed with a superior disdain. More than six decades after the Second World War we still tend to view Germany with a sceptical eye – never missing a chance to poke fun. And we still think that France should be grateful to us for its liberation – which it is not.

As a nation we also take delight in our commercial and economic success. In the boom decade of 1997–2007, politicians and the public lauded the rise of the City as it overtook New York as the world's most important foreign exchange and banking centre. The label 'Made in Britain', whether it is on a Burberry raincoat, a Marks & Spencer worsted suit or a pint of locally sourced organic milk, is a source of pride, too.

Yet, despite all this, we have become extraordinarily careless when it comes to ownership of assets. It is astonishing to think that down the decades we have sold off almost everything we associate with Britain's greatness, from our ports – the source of our maritime traditions – to the electricity companies which provide us with light and warmth. Distinctive red London double-decker buses now ply Trafalgar Square and the sights of the capital wearing the livery of Deutsche Bahn, the German rail operator.

It was not until the autumn of 2009, when the American food company Kraft bid for emblematic chocolate company Cadbury, that any awareness of foreign ownership of apparently British enterprises was kindled. A country of chocolate eaters woke up in indignation and remote members of the Cadbury family (who had not been involved in confectionary for generations) took to the airwaves to express their disgust. The issue of ownership, for a short time at least, jumped to the top of the political agenda.

No one could have been more pleased by the sudden upsurge of pride in Cadbury than me. As City Editor of the *Daily Mail* (and before that the *Guardian*) I had been a strident critic of foreign ownership for almost two decades. Both papers indulged my interest and allowed me to write widely on the subject. In the financial community my opposition and latterly that of the *Daily*

Mail to overseas ownership was regarded as a form of xenophobia. Communications advisers to the companies in the sights of overseas buyers let it be known to clients that the *Daily Mail's* views did not represent those of the wider business community and were a kind of foible. What the critics tended to forget is that the *Daily Mail* has more business readers than almost any other national newspaper. Moreover, the deluge of emails, letters and comments received from readers and business has been overwhelmingly supportive of our stand.

Nevertheless, the zeitgeist remained intact. As far as those in authority were concerned, in free and global markets the tide of capital was not to be stemmed. What was in the interest of global finance was also in the national interest, even if it meant boards responding to short-termism. Somehow, the contrast between the permanence of personal ownership – as in the nurture and care of land – and short-termism of the stock markets was not properly understood or debated.

There was little awareness of the command and control which is lost when national treasures, whether they be the department store Harrods or the chemical giant ICI, are disposed of to the highest bidder. It is the natural order of things that companies with headquarters overseas put their own interests first in much the same way as the gentry view keeping ownership of their land in the family as vital.

This book was inspired by the upsurge of interest in ownership triggered by the battle of Cadbury. But it seeks to probe deeper. It looks at the conditions which allowed Britain to become the favourite destination for overseas predators, the indifference of our policymakers, their neglect of our economic security and the impact on efforts to rebalance commerce in favour of making things after the financial panic of 2007–2009.

In bringing this endeavour to fruition I have been greatly helped by a number of people. My editor at the *Daily Mail* Paul Dacre has given me the freedom of the paper to write about selling Britain short. Associate City Editor Ruth Sutherland has adjusted her diary to help me in my book-writing activities and reinforced my views on the need to nurture manufacturing. City Office secretary Edwina O'Reilly assisted in the organisation of interviews.

This project was taken forward with great enthusiasm by Jonny Pegg of Jonathan Pegg Literary Agency who recognised the importance of the material. He turned, for the third time (after publishing *The Crunch* and *The Great Pensions Robbery*), to Nigel Wilcockson of Random House who embraced the idea warmly. As editor Nigel has been tough, thorough, sensible, meticulous and inspirational. I frequently hear from fellow authors of editors who show little interest in the narrative. Nigel is the opposite, taking an interest in every chapter and every draft.

I also owe a debt of gratitude to Norman Hayden, my collaborator for a trio of books, who undertook much of the early research on this project.

My family have also played a critical part. My wife Tricia has been with me all the way on this book which has disrupted family holidays in Majorca, Crete and at home. I cannot thank her enough. Other family members, notably Justin and Gabriel, technical teams always at hand to assist with computer, communications and research snags, also deserve credit.

My daughter Jessica, her husband Dan and their three children have taken a keen interest in this piece of work throughout.

Suffice it to say a book, with as much takeover detail in it as this, is bound to contain mistakes. Certainly, many of the bids and deals considered will have been viewed very differently by the participants from the interpretation presented here. There should be no doubt that responsibility for views expressed and any errors rests with me alone.

Alex Brummer, March 2012

Introduction

It was a crisp, typically autumnal morning when the eight-seater private jet landed at Luton Airport. It was immediately met by a chauffeur-driven limousine. The group stepping out of the £30 million Gulfstream G550 was led by a dark-haired, diminutive, trim and immaculately turned-out woman. To the casual eye she cut an unassuming middle-aged, middle-class figure. Dressed in a black suit, she looked like a mother comfortable with the school run, doing the weekly shopping or at a charity lunch with fellow fund-raisers.

Impressions, however, were misleading, for the woman slipping into Britain almost unnoticed on this particular day was the hard-headed boss of one of the world's major conglomerates. Indeed, as she arrived news broke that she had become second only to Michelle Obama – but ahead of Oprah Winfrey – on the Forbes' List of the world's most powerful women.

Irene Rosenfeld, Chairman and CEO of American corporate giant Kraft Foods, and the woman who bought Cadbury, was back in town.

Some eight months earlier her protracted struggle to take over Cadbury had finally ended in victory. The tough New Yorker, who owns to being a fan of Creme Eggs and Curly Wurlys, had landed the prize she wanted most. She believed Cadbury, whose chocolate and other confectionery brands were known the world over, could drive a stagnant Kraft Foods towards profitable growth, and was prepared to pay £11.5 billion to back her hunch.

In snapping up Cadbury, however, Rosenfeld had become a hated figure in Britain. Cadbury was regarded as a quintessentially British company with a proud Quaker legacy and a reputation for both business success and philanthropy. Kraft was viewed as an unworthy wooer, a foreign behemoth that was seeking to mask its struggle to grow by taking over a healthier company. Fears had been voiced about the risks a Kraft takeover might pose for Cadbury's future, for British jobs, and for Britain's overall economic health. These fears had seemed justified when Rosenfeld announced in February 2010 that Kraft would be closing Cadbury's Somerdale factory at Keynsham near Bristol and transferring jobs to Poland – having said in October 2009 that the factory would be kept open. In addition, the future of a key research and development base at Reading had been put in doubt. The commonly held view was that a foreign interloper such as Kraft was not to be trusted.

No doubt Rosenfeld was dwelling on all this controversy as she sped to Cadbury's spiritual heartland on 7 October 2010. People at Bournville weren't just worried about job security. The wider community had benefited from all that Cadbury had done over the years, using its chocolate wealth to fund schools and colleges, hospitals, convalescent homes, churches, housing and sports facilities. Would this all go with the takeover?

Ahead of Rosenfeld's arrival, a 3.5 per cent pay rise backdated to March had been announced, along with assurances that there would be no more compulsory redundancies for at least two years. She must have hoped that this would lead to a measure of good will.

She arrived at Bournville amid something of a 'publicity blackout' as to her precise movements. Looking energetic and enthusiastic, she stepped out of her car into a setting that reflected the subtly changing face of Bournville: the lamp posts outside the factory were still the famous Cadbury purple and the Union flag still flew, but in the reception area of the main building Kraft branding was beginning to edge its way in.

Rosenfeld did not talk to union representatives during her visit, preferring to meet management and a pre-selected group of employees. Orders went out that nobody should speak to the press, and by lunchtime rumours around Bournville were rife: one had it that Rosenfeld was meeting all staff at 3.30 p.m., while another suggested she had already gone back to the US.

Little is known of what was said at Bournville that day, although a question-and-answer session is thought to have taken place. While there, Rosenfeld took time to have lunch at the famous Cadbury World tourist attraction and reportedly served cucumber sandwiches and tea to residents of a Birmingham hostel. Then, her whistle-stop tour over, she left again, saying that she had been 'inspired' by what she saw. She was later reported as saying: 'We certainly understand that Bournville will remain at the heart and soul of our chocolate business and we are delighted about that. I think the key for us, though, is that this is a global business. We need to ensure that we are competitive on a global basis.'

Cadbury, with worldwide sales of £37 billion, certainly promised that.

The furore surrounding the Kraft takeover of Cadbury has subsided now. But the whole affair raised important questions – about British attitudes to home-grown businesses, about foreign involvement in British industry, about the future shape of the British economy – that are highly pertinent today. Britain is unique among developed nations in having a very relaxed attitude to foreign ownership. But is that the right view? In our pursuit of the banking and services sectors, have we turned our backs on manufacturing? Indeed, in an era of increasing economic uncertainty, ought we to be concerned that so much of our economy is no longer in our hands?

1

The Thatcher Revolution

In the early 1980s, in scenes unprecedented at that time for a major financial institution, trade unions formed picket lines outside branches of the Royal Bank of Scotland. It was the very public face of a wave of passionate national opposition to a takeover bid for RBS launched by the Hongkong and Shanghai Banking Corporation.

RBS had a venerable pedigree. Founded in 1727, it had pioneered the concept of the overdraft, printed its own banknotes and had occupied the same neo-classical stone headquarters on Edinburgh's Charlotte Square for two centuries.

By the early 1980s, however, the bank was faltering and had become vulnerable to a takeover. Its deposit base had grown handsomely on the back of the North Sea oil boom but Scotland itself offered few opportunities for major expansion; and RBS's English offshoot, the former Williams & Glyn's bank, was too small to make a real impact on the fast-changing UK, European and global banking scene. This was a new world where the biggest banks would club together to raise billions of pounds of syndicated loans for large multinational corporations and sovereign nations from Iran to Latin America. Smaller enterprises weren't players.

Recognising the bank's shortcomings, the group's board looked to seize the initiative by seeking a merger with a British bank with a large overseas presence. The apparently ideal candidate came in the form of Standard Chartered Bank – a bank with headquarters in London but most of its operations in Asia, the Middle East and Africa. A deal between the two parties would, it seemed, offer RBS the chance to create a truly international operation while continuing to be based in Edinburgh. Talks were therefore duly opened in 1980. When Standard Chartered Bank proposed a 'friendly' merger, the RBS board responded favourably and went on to make a public announcement in 1981. The outline terms were then approved by the Bank of England.

Within days, however, Hong Kong-based HSBC came forward with a rival offer and battle was joined. Trade unions were massively hostile. So, too, was much of Scotland's business, political and industrial elite. The Scottish Office voiced its opposition, as did the Scottish Development Agency, Scottish Nationalists, the TUC, the Labour Party and leading Edinburgh financiers and economists. All argued strongly that foreign ownership would erode Scotland's economic independence, lessen local career prospects and discourage the nation's entrepreneurs. Scotland, they argued, should be the home of an independent bank complete with a Scottish headquarters, rather than become part of the grand plan of another company and country. (The fact that the Hongkong & Shanghai Bank had a history of being run by single-minded Scots was not mentioned.)

Opposition didn't only come from Scotland. 'Not spoken aloud, but clearly below the surface,' an *Observer* journalist wrote, 'is a feeling that the secretive Hong Kong bank is perhaps a little too sharp and maybe not quite the proper sort of owner for a British clearing bank.' The Governor of the Bank of England Gordon Richardson was similarly opposed. He told HSBC chief Michael

Sandberg in no uncertain terms that his £498 million bid was 'unwelcome'. Among his fears was a worry that HSBC would not subject itself to the Bank's authority in the way that British-owned banks were obliged to do.

Faced by a public furore, and a governor of the Bank of England up in arms, Margaret Thatcher's government, which had come to power just two years before, felt it needed to act. It stepped into the fray and referred the two bids, the friendly offer from Standard Chartered and the hostile bid from HSBC, to the Monopolies and Mergers Commission. In January 1982 the MMC ruled against both, arguing that foreign dominance of the Royal Bank of Scotland would be against the public interest – even in the case of the proposed 'friendly' Standard Chartered deal.

Economic patriotism this may have seemed. But the failed bid for RBS turned out to be the last of its kind and marked a watershed in the history of who owns British business. The mood music surrounding foreign takeovers was about to change radically as Thatcher led a revolution that would open up the markets to all comers. Deregulation would see the unblocking of Britain's capital markets to overseas investment and the start of a takeover bonanza in which almost no major British firm – with the exception of a handful of defence manufacturers – would be immune to the advances of overseas groups.

In themselves mergers and takeovers were, of course, nothing new to the Britain of the early 1980s. The giant Imperial Chemical Industries (ICI), for example, was not the result of organic growth over many years but the product of a four-way merger between the giants Brunner-Mond, Nobel Industries, United Alkali and British Dyestuffs Corporation. Back in 1926 the leaders of the four companies had used the seclusion of a trip by liner to New York to hammer out a deal that provided Britain with a new chemicals and industrial conglomerate, conceived as a national champion that would fly the Union flag across the globe. Nor was foreign involvement in British enterprise previously unknown. America's General Motors – the home to brands Chevrolet, Pontiac and Cadillac – had rescued Britain's ailing Vauxhall Motors with a $2 million friendly bid as far back as 1925.

In the years after the Second World War, it was actually the government that led the way in the business of mergers and acquisitions. Britain's economy grew rapidly in the late 1940s as peaceful production took over from armaments and Britain found itself in demand as a global supplier of goods that ranged from steel to ships and from aircraft to chemicals. Clement Attlee's Labour government was convinced that bigger was better. It therefore amalgamated large swathes of the economy, including electricity and gas supply, the railways, aircraft production, airlines, steel manufacturing and even took the semi-independent Bank of England under state control. In a not dissimilar manner, the Conservative ministry that succeeded Labour examined the mass of small manufacturers involved in Britain's defence trade and decided that amalgamation was the way to build a world-beating business. The 1957 defence White Paper proposed the rationalisation of aircraft production to meet the demands of mounting research and development. At that time there were no fewer than 20 British aircraft manufacturers. By the early 1960s, with government encouragement, the number had shrunk to three main groups: Westland, for helicopters, Hawker-Siddeley and the British Aircraft Company (the future BAE Systems) which brought together the aerospace activities of English Electric, Vickers and Bristol Aircraft.

Harold Wilson's Labour government, which came to power in 1964, further drove forward the merger agenda with the creation of the Industrial Reorganisation Corporation, designed to build domestic firms capable of competing with overseas challengers. Run by the former boss of Courtaulds Frank Kearton it set about creating a series of industrial giants. Among those to emerge were Arnold Weinstock's GEC, ICL in computers and Swann-Hunter in shipbuilding. A rather less impressive example was the creation of Leyland from a combination of badly run volume car makers, including Austin Morris and Rover, and a bus and truck maker.

Government, business and the City alike largely beat the same drum in the 1950s and 1960s. Their aim was to make the UK better able to compete on a fast-changing global stage and to harness its considerable technological skills in everything from aerospace to computers. They wanted to create great competitive industries able to take on the multinationals that were choosing to base some of their European operations on these shores. Foreign involvement certainly wasn't ruled out. US car manufacturers Ford and General Motors, for example, were able to become embedded in the UK, bringing with them in the process American-style production line techniques. Nor was the UK blind to the potential for global free trade, as tariff barriers started to fall away, or to the potential for direct investment from abroad and by major multinationals.

Nevertheless, direct foreign involvement tended to be the exception rather than the rule. Bids and deals were carefully policed by the Monopolies and Mergers Commission (although it has to be admitted that its major preoccupation at this time was the potential for price-setting by big new companies rather than concerns about ownership). Moreover, capital controls meant that it was all but impossible for a foreign predator to grab control of a major British outfit, except in cases of acute distress where the stark choices were government subsidy for loss-makers, overseas ownership, or receivership. The American conglomerate ITT, for example, was permitted to gain a foothold in the UK consumer electrical market in the 1960s because it offered to step in to save struggling radio and television manufacturer Kolster-Brandes – which traded under the KB brand. In any other circumstances it is hard to believe that their bid would have been welcomed.

There was a problem, though: Britain's grand plans didn't work. By the early 1950s, the country was beginning to lag behind other industrial nations, including a re-emergent Germany and Japan. A decade later and things were no better. The United States, Japan, Germany and others were all increasingly challenging the UK on its home turf, in high growth sectors from cars to electrical engineering, from electronics to office machinery.

The fact that Britain had a Commonwealth to trade with was not enough to offset its difficulties. In the immediate post-war period when there was little competition from other industrial powers the UK economy looked robust enough. But as the infrastructure of the wartime foes was repaired, the shortcomings of Britain's lack of investment in new factories, plant and machinery was badly exposed. The UK's Victorian factories and pre-war machinery was no match for the German and Japanese embrace of the best new technology and machine tools.

Moreover, nationalisation of large parts of the British economy by the post-war Labour government proved counter-productive. The heavy hand of government weighed on these newly created industries, creating overmanned and unnecessarily bureaucratic companies. Things were scarcely made better by restrictive practices on the part of unions and by relatively high wage settlements. And there was a lack of investment: in a country where social security and the National Health Service were understandably highly valued, ministers competing in Cabinet for funds for nationalised enterprises found themselves at a disadvantage.

The private sector struggled too, undermined by a short-term attitude to investment and growth. Anglo-Saxon capitalism was a useful tool in concentrating owners but too many of the companies and their directors were insufficiently interested in long-term success. The tyranny of funding the rising dividend payout and buoying up the share price had a tendency to overwhelm all other goals.

Clearly, then, the creation of giant companies was not enough in itself to kickstart the economy. Advocates of takeovers would have argued, as they always do, that companies that grow through merger and acquisition are better able to compete on a global scale, that they can operate more cost-effectively and grab a larger share of the market. In reality, this didn't happen in the decades after the war – and in fact there's not much evidence that it works now.

The British approach contrasted strongly with those of such countries as Germany. There the presence of the Mittelstand, the vast collection of medium-sized businesses that have remained in family control for generations, produced a different form of capitalism focused on long-term survival rather than immediate gratification. The family element meant that firms were largely immune to tinkering of the kind undertaken in Britain and were more focused on investment. Japan operated a very different system too. There the 'integrated national system' placed the national interest above those of the individual or the investor. The result was a system of lifetime employment, seniority-based wages and consensus-based decision-making which allowed its great corporations to build inexorably and conquer new markets.

When Margaret Thatcher took power in 1979, she inherited an economy that was staggering badly. Repeated sterling crises, balance of payments deficits, strikes and soaring national debt had taken their toll. Inward investors were wary of the UK. They worried about its abysmal industrial relations record and were intimidated by the constant threat of IRA terrorism. It's scarcely surprising, then, that overseas ownership of UK firms stood at just 3.6 per cent – an all-time low.

Thatcher knew that something had to be done, but her initial approach was quite cautious. As Eric J. Evans noted in his book *Thatcher and Thatcherism*:

> Thatcher presented herself as someone passionate for change in order to rebuild Britain's morale . . . but she frequently relied upon canniness and caution which was a vital, if understated, part of her political make-up.

That said, while in opposition she had started to formulate a new philosophy that in time came to dominate her thinking: neo-liberalism. This was a term originally coined by the German economist Alexander Rüstow as far back as 1938, but it has largely come to be associated with the doctrines of the Austrian-born Friedrich Hayek, the twentieth-century economist turned political philosopher, whose magnum opus was *The Constitution of Liberty* – a book Thatcher famously banged down on the table at a meeting with her staff, saying: 'This is what we believe.'

Hayek and other leading economists like America's Milton Friedman were proponents of the small state, free markets and entrepreneurialism by deregulation. In each respect their views ran contrary to the received wisdom that had shaped post-war Britain. But they had influential supporters. Veteran Conservatives such as Enoch Powell and Sir Keith Joseph were enthusiastic economic neo-liberals. So, too, was Sir Alan Walters – who became Thatcher's economics guru – and Liverpool University's Professor

Patrick Minford. All had Margaret Thatcher's ear, and she came to rely on their arguments and insights.

Writing in the *New Statesman* in November 2010, the Labour grandee Lord Hattersley described the economic philosophy that emerged after Mrs Thatcher's election in 1979: 'Its defining principle was the efficacy of the market, as a guarantee of competitive efficiency and as a method of determining the allocation of resources and patterns of remuneration.' There was an evangelical force to it too. As the late American-born philosopher and thinker Shirley Letwin argued in her book *The Anatomy of Thatcherism*, the driving forces behind Thatcher's popular capitalism weren't just economic; they also included 'moral and social virtues'.

In practical terms three basic prongs of economic Thatcherism emerged: breaking the hold of trade unions, lifting the burden of government control over large parts of the economy's infrastructure, and unleashing the power of the individual. Things didn't happen overnight, nor were the first steps towards economic reform taken without considerable initial pain – the early 1980s saw a swift rise in levels of both inflation and unemployment. Nevertheless, the building blocks were gradually laid. Thatcher's own political convictions told her that nationalisation and government ownership of large sectors of the economy from power generation to airlines had been a terrible error. Public ownership was a burden which stymied innovation and initiative. It was not the job of government to run businesses. Moreover, selling off public assets promised to yield much needed government cash (and it wasn't without precedent: fresh in people's memories was the selling of 17 per cent of government shares in BP in May 1977 by James Callaghan's Labour government, at the behest of the International Monetary Fund and in order to raise a large sum of money quickly).

*

The early sell-offs, up to 1983, were relatively small-scale and tentative, one of the first being the science firm Amersham International, which arguably should never have been in state hands in the first place. It was sold for £70 million. Eventually, in 2003 the former state-owned group, with a reputation for medical innovation using nuclear technology, was to be sold to America's vast General Electric group for £5.7 billion. Unusually, GE Healthcare decided to fold its operations into Amersham, making it one of the few modern takeovers that brought with it genuine inward investment.

Next on the list was a small nationalised company, the National Freight Corporation (NFC). Proposals to privatise the NFC, set up originally by the Labour government of 1948, were contained in the Tories' 1979 election manifesto. The NFC had assets valued at £100 million. As a government-owned transport conglomerate it had swallowed several well-known logistics companies, including BRS, National Carriers, Roadline UK, Pickfords Removals, Pickfords Travel and Tempco International. NFC employed 26,000 people, and possessed 18,000 vehicles operating from 700 locations. It was Europe's largest single freight company and had about 10 per cent of the UK road haulage market. The company was sold to its management and the National Freight Consortium was established in February 1982. Seven years later it was floated on the London Stock Exchange.

The success of the NFC privatisation encouraged Thatcher to get after her bigger targets and the years 1983 to 1987 would prove to be the 'golden age' of privatisation. Revenue was still an important factor in driving things forward. Despite Thatcher's efforts to reduce public spending, higher unemployment meant that by 1983 the government's finances were deeply in the red, with a deficit of around 4 per cent of GDP. Constant injections of cash were needed.

But ideology became increasingly critical too. The Conservatives wanted to change Britain's political culture and popular capitalism became a buzzword. If people had a direct financial stake in the economy, it was argued, they would have a direct stake in its future success. It seemed a recipe for economic and social stability and progress.

One of the ways Mrs Thatcher stamped her authority on the free enterprise agenda was to chair the Cabinet sub-committee responsible for her government's early privatisations. This allowed her to retain control and micro-manage events. Asked about this, she likened her role to a coach-driver whipping the horses. She relied on her advisers, from the Treasury and her own policy unit, to make sure the horses felt the sting of the lash! She now knew that allowing private individuals to buy into the former state-owned businesses was a sure winner with a British public who liked a 'punt'. The government could set the price of shares in the previously nationalised industries and utilities and so virtually guarantee profits for small investors and bolster the public coffers at the same time.

The apparent success of privatisation in Britain saw the idea find a firm footing around the world. Government, administrative and legal teams were sent to London to study how it was done. On almost every continent, privatisation programmes would be set in motion. The expertise of the investment banks based in London provided a new and valuable stream of income for City firms. The UK's pioneering of privatisation was regarded in some quarters as Britain's biggest contribution to the political economy since the British economist John Maynard Keynes gave the world 'Keynesianism'.

Following the early successes, fundamental parts of the nation's infrastructure which had been in public ownership – energy, telecoms, water and other utilities – were offered for sale. The £4 billion disposal of British Telecom in 1984 engendered great public enthusiasm, its success exceeding Thatcher's wildest expectations. With the offer oversubscribed almost tenfold, the result was instant profit for the 2.3 million applicants.

In 1986 came the turn of British Gas and 14 regional public electricity suppliers who between them enjoyed a monopoly of gas and electricity supply to all domestic energy customers. An unashamedly down-market 'Tell Sid' advertising campaign sought out those who had never previously owned shares. The TV ads even managed to convince Labour's traditional voters that the government was handing out 'free' money. Some ten years later further deregulation of the energy markets would see consumers free, for the first time, to shop around for the best deal.

British Airways, viewed as an embarrassingly bloated national carrier which seldom showed a profit, was floated a year later. This came after a four-year struggle to sell it off, which had been stalled by American legal complications. It required the personal intervention of Thatcher to persuade President Reagan to end a Grand Jury investigation that threatened the offering.

BA was finally sold in February 1987 and would soon be transformed into one of the world's best and most profitable airlines. Also in the first half of that year, and on the back of a rip-roaring stock market, Rolls-Royce and British Airports Authority were floated successfully. The key role of Rolls-Royce in the defence of the realm, as a maker of the engines that powered the nation's fighter jets, meant it was largely ring-fenced from overseas predators. Indeed, it was not until 2011 that the company won the right to appoint a foreign chief executive or chairman if they turned out to be the best person on the job. Even though it ran the nation's airports BAA did not enjoy the same status and was to become a victim of one of the most widely disparaged foreign takeovers when it fell victim to a Spanish bid in 2006.

The de-nationalisation of the water industry was next, much of it, too, eventually ending up in overseas ownership. The sale meant that when Thatcher left office in 1990 only a rump of the old public sector remained. By the end of the decade 50 big companies had been sold or were scheduled for sale – more than two-thirds of the industrial assets owned by the state in 1979.

Unleashing entrepreneurship and freeing business from the shackles of government became almost an obsession and it happened at all levels. In Southend in Essex in the early 1980s the local borough council handed refuse collection and street cleaning to a private company, Brengreen, run by David Evans, who later became a Conservative MP. Evans's sales pitch was that council-delivered services were being run for the benefit of staff rather than ratepayers: Brengreen could do it cheaper and better. Word spread, and within a couple of years many more councils were contracting out refuse collection and street cleaning services.

At a national level, the sums raised from privatisation were substantial. It has been estimated that almost £19 billion was raised between 1979 and 1987. The sale of other publicly owned behemoths, such as British Rail and British Steel, followed. The latter, which lost more than £1 billion in its final years as a state concern, became the largest steel company in Europe after forging a merger with its Dutch competitor Hoogovens. As for the coal industry, John Major's government went on to sell off the remnants for £1 billion. Overall, in the 18 years of Conservative government up to 1997, over £60 billion of UK business assets were transferred from the state to the private sector. The proceeds vanished into the black hole of public spending.

The privatisation of key industries and assets was to have major repercussions later in terms of growing foreign ownership of previously British enterprises, but this would not have been possible if the privatisation drive had not been accompanied by an opening up of the City and of the financial sector generally.

The City had long been critical to the nation's prosperity, but in the course of the twentieth century it had increasingly lost the dominant position it enjoyed in Victorian times to Wall Street. By the 1960s and 1970s it seemed a rather archaic place with its strict dress code and old-fashioned business practices. Yet this was precisely the period when it experienced a renaissance. Irked by heavy-handed regulations on Wall Street, international finance started to flood back to London, encouraged by the Bank of England's very light monitoring of foreign banks. Over the next few years London became the centre for trading Eurodollars, Eurocurrency and Eurobonds. These comprised foreign holdings held outside the issuing country.

The City's appeal to overseas financiers included the depth of its markets, its long tradition as a financial entrepôt, its handy location in the time zone between America and the Far East and the fact that the language it traded in was English. Against that, however, were stacked its strict capital controls and the archaic structure of the banking system whereby gentlemen in top hats, working for a small group of institutions called the discount houses, would act as intermediaries between the banking system and the Bank of England. On the one hand the creation of the euromarkets in the 1970s and 1980s attracted enormous foreign deposits to London and saw new institutions settle in the City. On the other, the Square Mile, with its fusty traditions and rules, was ill-equipped to deal with the influx. Moreover, many of the UK old-style merchant banks – known as accepting houses because of their right to accept bills – were under-resourced to deal with the huge transactions that were part of an increasingly globalised marketplace.

Thatcher rightly recognised that, despite all its innate advantages, London was a stuffy place, hampered by old rules and the old ways of doing business, with an elitist 'old boy' network in charge. She wanted to see appointments based on talent rather than wealth and where you went to school. And she wanted a more freewheeling approach to business.

The first step taken was a cautious and apparently innocuous one. In Geoffrey Howe's sombre 1979 budget, the Chancellor announced his decision to relax exchange controls. From now on UK companies investing overseas were allowed to spend up to £5 million abroad without seeking permission from the authorities. At the same time restrictions on individuals travelling or living overseas were removed. It was an important symbolic gesture: in the past Britain had tended to look in on itself; now it was refocusing on the opportunities of the global marketplace and letting the rest of the world know that the country was a fully fledged member of the family of free market economies.

Initial fears that lifting the restrictions might trigger a sterling crisis proved unfounded. On the advice of Nigel Lawson – then financial secretary to the Treasury – the Chancellor subsequently went further than at first intended in the budget. Institutions were allowed to invest in foreign denominated currencies and restrictions on foreign direct investment were removed. A whole department at the Bank of England employing 750 people and responsible for enforcing exchange controls was closed down.

Most importantly the way was opened for cash to flow across borders and move in and out of the economy without hindrance. This, together with the 'Big Bang' reforms of 1986 – which ended the restricted practices on the stock market that made the City as much a closed shop as the unions – provided the incentive for money to move freely backwards and forwards across Britain's borders.

When I asked Lawson to reflect on the changes made in the 1980s in the course of a conversation in the handsome surroundings of the coffee room of the House of Lords in 2011, he was very clear about the key decision: 'the really new thing was the end of restrictions on capital'.

> One of the consequences is that companies get taken over. Nothing in life is all good and very little is all bad. I think in general, particularly for this country, to have minimum restrictions, to have maximum freedom is certainly beneficial globally. We benefit enormously because we had huge overseas assets ourselves and we are acquiring further overseas assets. I think it is arguable . . . but London, in my opinion, would not be the important global financial centre that it is [had restrictions on capital not been removed]. Clearly, we are number one in Europe and one of the top two in the world.

Geoffrey Howe's move, though highly significant, happened relatively quietly. Not so the events of Monday 27 October 1986, popularly known as Big Bang day. This was the day when many old City practices were swept aside, in particular the formal separation that had long prevailed between stockbrokers who bought and sold securities and stock jobbers who made the market. Such an approach had proved cumbersome, dealing systems antiquated and commission structures inflexible. Not to mention the fact that the British approach was different from the system in the US and was even out of step with London's own international securities business.

After Big Bang, London firms could trade as both principal and agent on the foreign share and Eurobond markets. What's more, other restrictive practices were also lifted. From now on, foreigners were to be allowed into the London securities market, as they had been already into banking and to a lesser extent insurance, in return for getting London into the same sort of dominant position in international securities as it was in banking. Over the previous two decades America's commercial banks had moved much of their fund-raising activities for overseas corporations and sovereign states to London to escape the Interest Equalisation Tax introduced by John F. Kennedy in 1963. The result was a ballooning of value of securities and loan origination in London through what became known as the Eurobond and Eurodollar markets. In 1981, a record-breaking year, more than $180 billion of Eurodollar loans was raised in the City of London. This was business that in the past would have been done on Wall Street.

The American banks now had a fresh opportunity to move into stockbroking, equity trading and mergers and acquisitions and could treat the City as a testing ground for the new financial order. Overseas ownership of London stockbrokers, jobbers and securities dealers was allowed for the first time. These far-reaching reforms helped to transform London into the world's leading financial centre. With the rules relaxed, the doors were flung wide open and foreign banks and dealing houses rushed through. 'The City had discovered a modern destiny as a hub of international finance,' commented the *Economist* magazine on the 20th anniversary of Big Bang in 2006.

Barclays chairman Marcus Agius, a veteran of key takeover battles from his years as a corporate financier at merchant bank Lazards, believes that Mrs Thatcher's belief in open markets was as much practical as ideological. Speaking to me from his capacious office in Canary Wharf, with a fantastic view over London's 2012 Olympic site, he argued:

> What Mrs Thatcher and her government saw and the City didn't see was that the information revolution meant that the small parochial nature of the City and its business was going to change. The world's going to move to 24-hour trading and everything is going to be hooked up together and when that happened small British institutions would not be able to compete. Citibank, Continental Illinois and the international banks were much bigger, much better at capitalising and in the case of the Americans more sophisticated.

To meet this challenge, Agius went on to observe, Thatcher gave merchant banks and stockbrokers freedom to 'come under one roof' in the hope it would produce 'a British champion. Without exception in every deal the amalgamation failed.' This left the door open for the overseas giants to eventually come in and take advantage of the newly opened financial borders.

The leading foreign-owned investment banks opened prestigious premises in London, including the American contingent Chase Manhattan, Salomon Brothers, Morgan Stanley, Bear Stearns, Merrill Lynch, J. P. Morgan, Lehman Brothers and Goldman Sachs. Alongside these were Germany's Deutsche Bank and Dresdner Bank and France's Société Générale and BNP

Paribas, plus the Swiss UBS. City stalwart David Buik, then MD of Babcock & Brown Money Markets, recalls that Goldman Sachs and Salomon Brothers aspired for greatness but had yet to achieve it in London. But along with J. P. Morgan, Morgan Stanley, Merrill Lynch and Lehman Brothers, they quickly went to the top of the pile, assisted by some high-profile takeovers of London financial houses.

Amid much hand-wringing, most of Britain's brokerages and merchant banks were bought by foreign investment banks. The late 1980s and 1990s saw many of the City's famous names disappear as their shareholders and partners were showered with cash by hungry European and US banks.

Among the great names to go was S. G. Warburg, which became part of the Swiss Banking Corporation (later merged into UBS). Flemings was bought by Chase Manhattan, broker James Capel by HSBC which also acquired Samuel Montagu as part of its takeover of Midland Bank. And eventually in the 2000s Cazenove, the most established of London broking houses with many of the FTSE 100 among its clients, would be folded into J. P. Morgan. The merchant banking arm of the blue-blooded house of Schroders was bought by Citibank.

Elsewhere, Morgan Grenfell fell to Deutsche Bank, while Barings was bought by ING (Netherlands), Smith New Court (the broking arm of N. M. Rothschild) succumbed to Merrill Lynch, as did Kleinwort Benson to Dresdner Bank. Only one of the sizeable and historic merchant banks N. M. Rothschild – assisted by the large earnings it made from Thatcher privatisations – remained strictly under family ownership linked to the other Rothschild banks across Europe through a Swiss holding company.

London was now playing host to far more foreign banks than any other financial centre and had the biggest slice of the foreign-exchange market. The City became the European headquarters for large US banks as well as providing a major base for leading European banks. Business was gravitating to the City because its role was based no longer on sterling but on offshore currencies, predominantly dollars, held outside America. Banks from around the world were represented, with the Moorgate district alone nicknamed 'the Avenue of the Americas'.

American investment bankers brought a brash new style to London's financial markets. The City was transformed. Gone were the old ways: new social habits, sense of dress and informality began to predominate. The old 'late start, long lunch and early finish' mentality was swept away. Longer hours, shorter lunches and bigger pay were now the norm. British Rail had to lay on new services to get City workers from Surrey and the other Home Counties to their desks by 7 a.m. They then arrived to giant new trading floors replete with banks of computer screens. Under the remorseless American influence, sales of bottled water soared, while the gym replaced the pub at lunchtime.

As London prospered, it drew closer and closer to New York. Money, people and ideas flowed back and forth between the two great cities. With nothing to restrict them, investment houses began to shape City life by offering Wall Street salaries and bonuses – often based on risky practices, as would later emerge in the global banking meltdown from 2007. In some instances, London law firms had to double what they paid newly qualified lawyers because of pressure from the New York competition.

Even dress codes were affected, as City boys began wearing chinos and shirts open at the neck. It was not uncommon for those who could afford it to own homes in both cities. More money was churning through London and New York than through all the rest of the world's financial centres combined.

London-based American journalist Stryker McGuire recalls:

A new generation of 'masters of the universe' replaced the less inventive and less aggressive pinstriped stockbrokers and bankers of old. London was the centre of this revolution in British life. The City was perhaps the single greatest driver behind the prosperity and laissez-faire gumption that cascaded across the country.

With even more overseas banks flooding in, the City burst eastwards from its former boundaries around the old 'Square Mile' and redrew the capital's skyline. Canary Wharf, previously a wasteland in East London's Docklands, sprouted skyscrapers, including Britain's tallest, that came to provide palatial premises for global banks with giant trading floors. Within 20 years almost as many financial staff worked in this one area as in the whole of Frankfurt, London's main European rival. Highly paid traders, financiers and other professionals flooded in.

As banks expanded and consolidated, they started to offer a wider array of products and services to a growing market. This brought new entrants into the financial markets and accelerated the dynamics of institutional change. The flood of mergers and acquisitions activity in the 1980s in the industrial sector spread to the financial sphere once the potential benefits of restructuring could be realised in a more open regulatory climate. At the same time, controls on spending limits and conditions for credit were loosened and, in many cases, removed. Companies were allowed to develop new products, and barriers that previously restricted a bank's ability to diversify were also lifted.

The globalisation of trading that accompanied the growing integration of the world economy also had a hand in the consolidation. Banks and other lenders were soon moving into each other's national territories. Centres such as Tokyo and Frankfurt benefited. They were helped in this by the decision taken by central banks in the late 1980s to bring in minimum international regulatory standards. They were also aided by dramatic improvements in the speed and quality of telecommunications, computers and information services that helped to lower information costs and other aspects of completing transactions for the financial institutions.

Some retail banks even tried setting up integrated investment banking operations – not always successfully – as Barclays found with its Barclays de Zoete Wedd (BZW) experiment in the 1990s. Building societies changed too. A provision of the Financial Services and Building Societies Acts of 1986 effectively abolished the limitations on the ways that building societies raised funds. Previously they had been restricted to raising funds from individual members' deposits. Now they could operate far more widely, and the result was that the dividing line between UK banks and building societies became blurred. Building societies could become banks if 76 per cent of members voted in favour, at which point they would drop their 'mutual' status and become a limited company. Abbey National kicked things off by becoming a public limited company (plc) in 1989. Eight other building societies followed suit in the 1990s. Other societies merged, or linked up with banks, such as the Trustees Savings Bank combining with Lloyds to form Lloyds TSB.

As building societies demutualised and went private, power passed from members to shareholders, such as overseas institutions. Some building societies which became banks were eventually to be foreign owned: Abbey, for example, became part of Spanish giant Banco Santander, which also stepped in to rescue the former mutuals Alliance & Leicester and Bradford & Bingley that had been destabilised by the 2007–2008 financial crisis. Similarly, through a series of mergers some building societies and smaller banks also fell under foreign ownership.

The Bristol & West building society fell under the ownership of the Bank of Ireland, which was badly damaged by the 2010–2011 sovereign debt implosion. Clydesdale Bank and Yorkshire Bank were taken over by the National Australian Bank. The deregulation of the financial system broke down the traditional barriers between the building societies and the banks and opened the doors to overseas ownership of previously independent, regionally based institutions. In the process mutually owned societies, like Bristol & West, became the anonymous subsidiaries of large foreign-owned financial conglomerates with no particular national or regional loyalties.

In fact, a powerful overseas presence in the UK became very much a hallmark of the financial sector after Big Bang. Before 1914, 30 foreign banks were established in London. By 1987 that number had rocketed to 434 – a growth of more than fourteen-fold. American banks alone employed 21,000 people in the City. From the mid-1980s both London and New York became home to more foreign than domestic banks, the City actually holding the largest slice of the foreign exchange market. It was a classic example of an economic cluster, whereby businesses locate close to one another because they gain from proximity. 'The big warehouse of markets is in London,' Pascal Boris, Chief Executive of French bank BNP Paribas's British operation wrote on the *New Economist* website in 2006.

Not everyone thinks that this was necessarily a move in the right direction. Critics have argued that deregulation aided the very foreign – mainly American – investment banks at the expense of home-grown institutions. They also suggest that while a more US-style business culture has made the City more diverse, it has also made it more cut-throat and more prepared to take short cuts and big risks. Regulatory indulgence fostered the exploitation of smart new financial products – including the toxic assets at the heart of the 2007–2008 great panic. The financial sector became based on an American-style fee and bonus-driven culture totally out of step with the earnings and expectations of the rest of the country's workforce. The bonus culture, which first emerged in the late 1980s, came increasingly to the fore, rewarding people even when their results didn't seem to justify the money they were scooping up.

For those critical of this style of doing business, the global financial meltdown that began in 2007 can be laid at the door of American investment banks whose hunger for constant increased profit led them to adopt unethical or even unlawful methods. At the height of the financial panic, in January 2008, one letter in the London *Evening Standard* claimed: 'Most organised crime committed in Britain has its origins abroad. Don't forget that 90 per cent of investment banks are foreign owned, and the damage these institutions are doing to you and me is far greater than a few gangs selling drugs to a willing public.'

There is another side to this argument, though. Over time, the financial and related business services industry became an increasingly important part of the British economy. 'The financial services industry is the largest sector of the economy,' says Andrew Cahn, chief executive of UK Trade and Investment, the government agency that promotes exports and inward investment. 'It's worth around 9 per cent of gross domestic product and growing twice as fast as the economy as a whole.' He adds: 'The City is, to all intents and purposes, foreign-owned – and it's all the better for it.'

Even after the crunch and the panic of 2007 and 2008, London in 2009 still hosted 254 foreign banks, enjoyed over 34 per cent of the world's foreign exchange market and more than 50 per cent of the global trade in foreign equities. At the same time, foreign businesses, whether Russian or Middle Eastern, who sought an overseas flotation, flocked to London for a Stock Exchange listing. In 2011 London hosted the $61 billion flotation of Swiss-based commodity and natural resources group Glencore, which came to the market creating five billionaires and dozens of millionaires in a single day. Glencore chief executive Ivan Glasenberg emerged from the launch with a net worth in excess of $10 billion.

The one part of the City that has remained resolutely in British hands is the London Stock Exchange itself. Over the past decade it has successfully fended off overseas ownership, rejecting bids from Deutsche Borse, NASDAQ in the United States, OMX in Sweden and the Australian private equity bank Macquarie in quick succession. Ironically its independence has only ultimately been possible because it opted to take strategic investors from Qatar and Dubai onto its books.

Foreign involvement or ownership in the financial sector, then, has been seen as both a blessing and a curse. On the minus side, it has led to a loss of control and the ascendancy of an approach to capitalism that has not been without its problems. On the plus side, it has brought in much-needed business and investment from abroad. 'We have a myriad of different businesses, types of people, cultures and nationalities that create the diversity necessary to compete globally and to develop new products and services,' Sir Michael Snyder, chairman of the Policy and Resources Committee of the City of London, told the *Financial Times* in 2007.

Arguably, the City's success rests on its openness as a financial market where ownership no longer matters. The very fact that open capital markets in the UK have made British business more susceptible to foreign ownership has simultaneously ensured the success of the City. The short-term benefits have proved enormous in terms of cementing London's place as the world's busiest financial centre and in turn creating jobs, wealth and rich streams of taxation for the Exchequer. But over the longer haul, as the 2010 coalition government would come to recognise, the economy had tipped too far in favour of finance and would need to be rebalanced in favour of manufacturing and other activities.

The openness of Britain's capital markets has also transformed ownership of enterprises that lie far beyond the confines of the Square Mile. Successive Conservative governments in the 1980s and 1990s presided over a greater than ten-fold rise in the proportion of British companies with foreign parents. Famous names such as the car makers Rolls-Royce and Bentley, the confectioner Rowntree, the chemical giant ICI, retailers Harrods, Hamleys, Fortnum & Mason and travel firm Thomas Cook, all quintessentially British, passed to international ownership.

Many of the great privatisations of the Thatcher era, designed in part to make the UK a nation of share owners, became over time foreign enterprises. When Margaret Thatcher became prime minister there were 3 million private shareholders in the UK. The number had risen to 11 million by the time she stepped down. But many were only in it for the short term, and as they parted with their shares to make a quick profit, so these shares passed into foreign ownership. Thatcher herself was aware of this possible outcome: in the early 1980s she tried to prevent control passing to foreigners through shares retained by the government – the so-called 'Golden Share'. But in 1989, after the proportion of foreign shares in British companies had quadrupled, she felt obliged to bow to the logic of the markets. From now on, foreign bids were allowed for all but the most strategically sensitive defence and nuclear enterprises (even this caveat was to crumble when the state-controlled French energy group Electricité de France was allowed to buy the nuclear generator British Energy in 2008).

Of course, trade went the other way too. Hanson, the conglomerate founded by two swashbuckling British entrepreneurs Lord (James) Hanson and Lord (Gordon) White is a case in point – and a corporation that very openly sold itself to shareholders as: 'The company from over here that's doing rather well over there.' Its logo consisted of two knotted scarves, one a Union flag and the other Old Glory, the American flag. During my period in the US, I watched Hanson complete a series of audacious American takeovers, including those of the chemical-to-typewriters group, SCM, the coal miner Peabody, Kaiser Cement and the house builder Beazer.

And Hanson was not alone. The Australian newspaper tycoon Rupert Murdoch, who had moved his centre of operations to Britain where he owned the *Sun* and the *News of the World* (which closed in 2011), began his search for a bigger canvas. In adding his first American newspaper titles to his portfolio – including the *New York Post* and *Boston Herald* – Murdoch attracted the anger of no less a figure than the late Senator Edward Kennedy, who tried to stop the deals by launching in congress a Bill of Attainder (a piece of legislation aimed at one person).

Among Murdoch's other American conquests was the publishing empire HarperCollins and Metromedia, a chain of seven big city television stations, which would eventually form the basis of his Fox media conglomerate – a challenger to the power of the 'big three' networks.

A key British-based swashbuckler was the late tycoon Sir James Goldsmith. So broad were his ambitions that at one point he was summoned before Congress to defend his assault on a raft of American companies, including the Connecticut-based conglomerate Continental Group, the forest products concern Crown Zellerbach and the tyres manufacturer Goodyear. His exploits and defence of capitalism were later featured, in lightly disguised form, in the 20th Century Fox movie *Wall Street* released in 1987.

In a less overtly aggressive way, British retail chains including Marks & Spencer also sought to plant a flag abroad. M&S, with mixed results, bought the preppie US clothing firm Brooks Brothers and Peoples Stores in Canada, while J. Sainsbury purchased the American chain Kings Supermarkets. All the major banks experimented with ownership of US financial groups: Midland Bank's purchase of Crocker National in California almost landed it in the bankruptcy courts.

Deregulation, then, helped open up markets and create an aggressively competitive global playing field in which Britain proved a significant player. It also made British companies much more vulnerable to foreign takeover – and the next few years were to see a flurry of takeover activity.

2

The Great Financial Free-for-All

The Thatcher reforms made the UK market the most open in the world. Other nations created a superstructure of rules, regulations and laws designed to refine, slow and test the flow of capital across their borders: restricting foreign shareholdings in certain activities from airlines to defence, for example; instituting special taxes to keep certain financial deals such as overseas bond issues at bay; limiting hedge funds and speculative transactions. Such limitations were not to be found in Britain. Overseas investors were therefore inevitably attracted to the UK. At the same time Thatcher's privatisation revolution which shifted ownership of many companies from the public to the private sector put a whole swathe of business within reach of foreign owners.

British companies had attractions to foreign buyers that went beyond their accessibility. Many were already global players with commanding positions in world markets, offering obvious benefits to would-be purchasers. They were generally attractively priced, holding out the potential for deals that were both earnings- and value-enhancing to shareholders. Multinational companies seek to invest where they see a mix of low costs, skilled and flexible labour markets and a competitive tax regime. Overseas firms found these features in abundance in Britain. Free movement of capital, flexible labour markets and a plethora of well-established enterprises gave the UK a unique selling proposition and offered a real competitive advantage.

In themselves, though, these factors might not have been quite enough to make the country's blue-chip companies and most-prized assets a target for overseas predators. What tipped the balance in the late 1990s and 2000s were three key factors: relatively cheap finance (debt finance was cheaper than it had been for 25 years); liberal takeover rules; and the presence of global investment banks in the City, with ready access to the world's capital.

Throughout the boom years of the late 1990s and early 2000s global investment houses were essentially allowed to write their own regulatory rules. Once it would have been considered risky for a bank to lend ten times its own share capital. At the peak of the credit boom in around 2005 the boldest and least risk averse of the banks – such as New York's Lehman Brothers – thought it fine to lend 45 times the bank's capital.

In retrospect, this seems the height of foolishness, but at the time it looked the obvious thing to do. The lender would get fat arrangement fees, use its mergers and acquisitions department to provide advice on the structure of the deal and establish a new source of income from interest flows and capital repayments. With a bit of luck, the borrower would come back a year or so later and want to restructure the finances, so creating yet another layer of fees. With seemingly unlimited amounts of cash available, and the financial regulators operating in a very hands-off way, some of the biggest firms in the world could become takeover targets. Leverage made everything seem possible.

There was also a very short-term view of major deals. It did not matter if the buyer was a foreign company such as Kraft Foods or a vigorous private equity fund like Blackstone. If the price was good enough, shareholders would take the money and run. So, too, would directors: many chief executives demanded that clauses be added to their contracts guaranteeing that if the firm they ran was taken over, the share options they had been granted – even those intended only to pay out over the long term – could be converted immediately and in full into cash.

The days when bids would be automatically halted by the Competition Commission – the successor to the old Monopolies and Mergers Commission – were long gone. Keen to keep in with big business and determined to ensure that Britain stayed at the centre of global finance, the Blair–Brown government that came to power in 1997 was anxious not to step in anyone's way.

And there were plenty of potential buyers in line for UK-based companies and assets. In Europe – or more precisely within the EU – a period of austerity, restructuring and severe cost-cutting had, by 2000, given way to a boom, bolstered by strong cash reserves. Corporate balance sheets were strong. The dawn of the single currency also meant that the less financially rigorous nations of Southern Europe, such as Spain, could take advantage of the low interest and stronger credit ratings of Germany and its northerly neighbours. Companies within the eurozone had the luxury of a choice of strategies: they could go for organic expansion by reinvesting directly in themselves or they could opt for growth by acquisition.

Further afield, the rise of the emerging market economies, most notably the BRIC economies of Brazil, Russia, India and China, opened the opportunity for an additional group of predators. These were nations which had seemingly won their three-decade struggle against inflation and were on the lookout for new opportunities. Many of these nations – particularly in Asia – were also by now operating with huge surpluses, fed by the Western hunger for their goods. In fact, this period saw a tremendous transfer of wealth from the Western democracies such as the United States to China, Taiwan, Singapore and others. A similar situation developed in the euro area where the powerhouses of the north such as Germany built rich surpluses, while those in the Mediterranean south – like Greece – ran on borrowing and debt.

Many of the surplus countries, most notably China, which by 2011 had built up reserves of an estimated $3 trillion, held on to large amounts of the cash rather than encouraging domestic consumption which would have recycled the money into the global economy. As a result, the deficit countries created ever-larger amounts of government and bank debt to finance their needs. Rather than leaving this debt sitting directly on their balance sheets as they had done in the past, Western banks chose to recycle it by financing takeovers. They became evermore creative in their establishing of new financial instruments. Many of the loans were packaged up, turned into debt securities and sold on to other banks, insurers and pension funds. This form of finance, known as securitisation or structured debt, was at the root of the US mortgage meltdown leading to the financial crisis of 2007–2009. It was also to play its part in the takeover boom.

The terrorist attacks on the Twin Towers of the World Trade Center in New York had a major impact on how the world economy evolved after September 11, 2001. For a brief moment, as the late (Lord) Eddie George, then governor of the Bank of England, admitted shortly afterwards, international finance nearly came to a halt. Confidence collapsed, and the spectre of recession raised its head as people grappled to comprehend a world that now seemed so dangerous and unstable.

Acutely aware of imminent disaster, Alan Greenspan, chairman of the Federal Reserve Board, America's central bank, acted quickly and decisively, lowering official American interest rates to just 1 per cent. Other central banks, including the Bank of England, followed suit.

The results were dramatic. Far from ushering in a crash, 9/11 actually led to a boom. Cheap credit suddenly seemed on tap to everyone. This was most clearly manifested to ordinary consumers in the housing markets on both sides of the Atlantic, where cheap mortgage finance helped stoke a boom that was ultimately to prove unsustainable.

But corporations benefited too, and found themselves in a strong position to pursue expansion agendas through acquisitions. The herd instinct, which so often drives financial markets, played its role. Corporations felt pressure to gear up their balance sheets with more debt and leverage than had previously been acceptable. Big investors positively encouraged companies to load up their accounts with debt finance and to use the cash to expand globally. Britain, with its open capital markets and 'grown-up' view of overseas takeovers, was no exception.

This heavy reliance on debt and leverage to finance growth became the hallmark of the post-9/11 era. It certainly wasn't a new technique. Traditionally, however, and particularly in the 1980s and 1990s, companies throughout the world had tended to use paper – their own shares – to make acquisitions: it was seen as the cheapest way of doing deals. Now that interest rates were so low, however, paper deals became unfashionable, increasingly resisted by existing investors who feared that the shares they held would be diluted in value should the company acquired fail to perform as promised. Instead, now that banks had seemingly endless supplies of money to lend at cheap rates, debt became the preferred attack weapon, with leverage – high levels of borrowing – the new buzzword.

Cheap and easy credit wasn't just easy to obtain; it often proved a much simpler route to securing a takeover than the shares option. By borrowing billions from the banks, the acquiring companies could overwhelm investors with promises of instant cash returns. Indeed, even the mere rumour of a takeover could generate rewards, as was later to be seen with Kraft's takeover of Cadbury in 2010 when short-term speculators such as hedge funds moved in for an easy kill and quick returns.

The new approach was fast too. Because the lure of cash was so strong, investment banks came up with ways of circumventing what had previously often been a long drawn-out takeover process through a court-approved 'scheme of arrangement' which allowed deals to be completed quickly. Such was the relentless momentum of a takeover bid made in this way that any opposition could be crushed by what amounted to shock and awe tactics. And no asset was immune from leveraged deals – from stellar football clubs like Manchester United, to major infrastructure firms such as the British Airports Authority and industrial groups like ICI, they were all there for the taking.

The use of debt finance was made even more advantageous by a tax system that favoured debt over equity. If a transaction was financed by debt then the interest on the loans could be charged against profits, so lowering the corporation tax bills for the acquiring firm. In the case of private equity takeovers of public companies, the tax arrangements were even more favourable. The interest on the debt raised by private equity companies for takeovers could be offset against corporation tax on future profits. The private equity partners were rewarded by what was known in the trade as 'carried interest' – the earnings on future profits when the assets were sold on. This was levied at the rate of capital gains tax (18 per cent to 28 per cent in 2010–2011 in the UK) against up to 50 per cent for income taxes.

And deals financed by debt offered financial excitement in an era when low interest rates and low inflation ensured superior returns that were unlikely to be found elsewhere. This calculation lay at the heart of the sub-prime housing boom. Would-be house-owners who traditionally could probably not have afforded a mortgage found themselves signing up to superficially attractive deals that then enveloped them in a high-interest debt. In a not dissimilar way, shareholders, companies, hedge funds and private equity groups desperately sought out debt-financed deals that could yield better returns than those on offer from traditional investments. Everyone seemed to gain. For executive directors, the micro-class of top managers who run companies, deals allowed them to cash in share options, provided under incentive schemes, which otherwise might take several years to mature. For bankers, deals offered the promise of fat fees. What's more, they could also then set repayment interest rates above market rates.

As for private equity firms, they would use debt financing to pounce on what they believed to be an under-performing firm. They would then resell the company or assets purchased at a higher price. Many specialised in the 'quick flip' – a short period of ownership when costs would be cut, the management smartened up and the company returned to the stock market at a big profit.

And the government loved it all too. So far as New Labour was concerned, the financial community was a wonderful source of tax revenues which could help finance reforms of education, health and other domestic priorities. Its short-term attitude to where the money was coming from and the true price being paid for it chimed well with the City's own philosophy.

A classic example of the aggressive new approach to takeovers was the 2003 deal whereby the department store group Debenhams, which had been trading since 1813, was bought by two US-based private equity firms, CVC Capital and Texas Pacific. The firm was stripped of cash and investment, loaded with debt, and returned to the stock market less than three years later at a big profit for the American owners in what turned out to be an enfeebled condition from which it never fully recovered.

The debt versus equity debate has been a core issue in finance for decades. In periods of low interest rates, the pendulum swings firmly toward debt. Indeed, in the 2000s the shares of companies which expanded through debt, making what analysts would call more efficient use of the balance sheets, were rewarded for their effort: the more 'highly geared' (borrowed) the balance sheet of these companies, the better the returns. The debt addiction, fuelled by accommodating monetary policy, was a characteristic of the period. Consumer debt soared in the UK during the first decade of the twenty-first century until it matched the size of the economy. There was a parallel increase in corporate debt and as the decade advanced, government debt also spiralled, despite the fiscal rules that were meant to constrain its expansion.

So, in the post-9/11 era the key attraction of debt for corporate Britain and America was that it was generally cheaper than fundraising through equities and it also offered management more flexibility – especially as the companies were not required to consult shareholders over such arrangements. It was popular with institutional investors who disliked seeing their equity (share) holding diluted and could enjoy the higher profits and dividends. Debt finance also provided a degree of certainty about future interest rate costs in a way that short-term finance, such as overdrafts, could not. Fixed-rate loans, taken out at times of low interest rates, meant that future financing costs could be forecast and planned for. Even variable rate loans looked to be less risky than in the past because there was a belief that the world had entered an era when interest rates would remain relatively low and the banks would always be willing to rollover or renew existing loans.

Moreover, the fashion for measuring the success of companies, particularly those in the fast growth, high-tech era in terms of EBITDA (earnings before interest, taxation, dividend and amortisation), meant that there was little downside to having a big interest rate bill. In fact, EBITDA earnings drove share prices higher than would have been the case had more traditional measures of post interest and tax profits been used.

Debt became so popular that some companies, most notably the former Welsh Water utility Glas Cymru, was restructured as an entity financed almost entirely by borrowings. Such a structure was particularly suited to a regulated utility where both current and future income is relatively stable and easily predicted.

But Glas Cymru is the exception rather than the rule. Generally speaking, debt alone makes for a fragile capital structure, as many companies came to realise when the credit crunch struck in 2007. In the 'NICE decade',[1] 1996–2006, the traditional demands for solid collateral were often less than rigorous and many loans, particularly to private equity, were made on the promise of future earnings flows. When the credit crunch and recession brought the economy to a shuddering halt in 2007–2009, property values

---

[1] In a speech in June 2006, the governor of the Bank of England Mervyn King coined the term 'NICE decade' (Non-Inflationary Continuous Expansion), referring to the years 1996–2006.

slumped and profits were crushed, destroying much of the collateral at the same time.

Debt also imposes more obligations than equity, because in most cases there is a requirement to pay back the principal and the interest. In the free and easy credit days of the early 2000s this wasn't too big a problem. Banks discarded their traditional caution and invented curious and unstable structures that blurred the ultimate responsibilities of the borrower. When, for example, the American Malcolm Glazer bought England's most famous football club, Manchester United, in 2005, most of the £800 million required did not come from him but was cash borrowed and secured against the club's assets. Part of the purchase price was in the form of payment in kind loans (known as PIKs) by which, instead of paying interest, the cost of borrowing is added to the principal. By March 2010, the PIKs loans accumulated by Manchester United stood at £107 million and had been sold on to hedge funds. The complex, newfangled financing provides a graphic example of the volatile structures used during the debt-fuelled NICE decade and the heavy risks involved.

Of course, borrowed money, and the interest on it, ultimately has to be paid back even if fancy structures such as PIKs postpone the deadline. Repayment is eventually required irrespective of the performance of the companies or assets purchased or the state of the underlying economy. The foolishness of undisciplined debt structures was exposed when credit dried up in 2007–2009 and banks demanded their money back, refinancing and a share of the equity as collateral.

Financing a deal by equity, in contrast, offers the promise of greater stability and can be shaped to meet changing economic and business conditions. Dividends to the equity shareholders tend to be delivered only when companies are in profit. In times of trouble, even the most prosperous firms will hold or even cut the dividend distribution to conserve cash. The market value of the equity in companies tends to rise if the business is doing well and has a robust future outlook. By the same measure, in times of trouble, it is the equity holders who have to pick up the pieces through new shares in the shape of a rights issue.

One way of restoring the balance sheets in the aftermath of the financial crisis of 2007–2009 was for companies to seek new funds in the shape of an initial public offering, known as a flotation, on the stock market. Some British assets that were sold to overseas buyers at the peak of the debt-fuelled boom returned to the London Stock Exchange later. In June 2011, for example, debt-ridden Dubai-based DP World, which had acquired British port operator P&O in 2006 for £3.92 billion, returned to the public markets with a listing which valued the enterprise at £6.1 billion, having added its Jebel Ali and other port assets to those originally owned by P&O. The finance raised by the public flotation enabled the group to pay down its debt burden as well as raise capital for future expansion. In what was largely a financially driven exercise, P&O ports had moved through a full circle, though in effect the ports company had been weakened by under-investment and was now controlled from Dubai rather than London.

As a rule of thumb, analysts tend to use a company's debt to equity ratio as the measure of the amount it is safe to borrow over long periods of time. The ratio is calculated by looking at the company's total debt – adding together short-term and long-term obligations – as a percentage of its equity. The higher the percentage of debt to equity, the more leveraged, or geared up, the company is seen to be. In times of strong economic output, high gearing is seen as an advantage because it drives growth. But, of course, it can prove problematic in bad times when credit conditions change, as the Glazer family, DP Ports, the Spanish group Ferrovial – the owners of BAA – and other foreign owners of UK companies all found to their cost.

Over the years, what has been regarded as an acceptable level of debt to equity has shifted, depending on both economic factors and society's general attitude to credit at any given period. Nevertheless a good rule of thumb is that any debt to equity ratio exceeding 40 per cent to 50 per cent leverage needs to be closely scrutinised to ensure that cash flow is adequate to meet interest and debt repayment schedules over time.

In the NICE decade that necessary scrutiny disappeared as private equity barons, overseas predators and investment banks, all keen to do deals, naively assumed that there was a new paradigm and that in an age of cheap and available credit there could be no danger. It was the sort of self-delusion that legendary economist J. K. Galbraith, talking about the build-up to the Great Crash of 1929, described as the 'bezzle'. 'Debt is the new equity,' declared Ryanair's Michael O'Leary as he used borrowed money to build a huge new fleet for his 'no frills' carrier. In his case, he was only able to keep his head above water as conditions became more difficult by passing on costs to his airline's passengers.

For those not involved in high finance, the dangers of building up high levels of debt might seem self-evident. But, of course, the risks were being taken at a time when there had been several years of uninterrupted economic growth. People forget all too quickly what happens when boom turns to bust – as it inevitably will. And the tax breaks made the debt route to financing irresistible.

Changing the tax system so it does not unduly favour debt over equity might seem the obvious way to remove a cause of systemic risk. Certainly, it would make it less easy for London-based banks to syndicate the loans that provide foreign enterprises with the cash to buy out well-known UK companies. A classic example of this turn of events came in 2009 when Kraft's purchase of Cadbury was part-funded to the tune of £630 million by the semi-nationalised Royal Bank of Scotland, in which the government owns an 84 per cent stake. As Liberal Democrat leader Nick Clegg put it in the course of a Commons debate on 20 January 2010: 'When British taxpayers bailed out the bank, they would never have believed that their money would be used to put British people out of work. Isn't that plain wrong?'

Clegg was not the only politician to have his doubts. In opposition, the Tory Shadow Chancellor George Osborne favoured removing the tax prejudice in favour of debt as part of a broader assault on tax breaks for corporate Britain. But in government, faced with the lobbying by business interests, he found it difficult to turn his misgivings into action.

For a range of reasons, then, debt became popular and risk correspondingly escalated. But there was also another dangerous element in all this: complexity. Debt is an easy enough concept to grasp, but when sliced, diced and bundled into apparently neat packages it becomes very slippery. Throughout the early years of the twenty-first century, loans were not kept straightforward but were endlessly repackaged and sold on, following methods first introduced in the US banking and credit system in the 1970s.

The housing market is perhaps the best-known example of the excesses of securitisation, home mortgages in the US being pooled by American government-backed agencies such as Fannie Mae and Freddie Mac (both of which were effectively nationalised in the summer of 2008). But securitisation was not confined to the housing market. In its increasingly complex forms it became a form of finance adapted and used across credit markets for everything from car financing, to student loans, to large-scale syndicated loans put together for big commercial deals. Such techniques gave the banks a new option for expanding lending, even in times of monetary constraints.

In the process good, solid loans with proper asset backing and made at the right price became virtually indistinguishable from poorly secured speculative loans. Indeed until the credit crunch in 2007, the broader public was barely aware of the scale of financial engineering that was going on. Over time securitisation came to fuel the credit boom, contributing to the surging profits of the big banks, the bonus culture and apparently ballooning profits. The complex derivative financial products on offer were rightly described by Warren Buffett, the Sage of Omaha and the world's most respected investor, as 'WMDs' (weapons of mass destruction).

The global monetary system of the early years of the twenty-first century thus came to resemble a giant Ponzi scheme when one investor is rewarded not from profits, but from money paid out by other investors. The derivatives bubble, housing bubble, debt-financed national spending plans and debt-fuelled takeovers were made possible by a fiat currency – that is, paper money backed by nothing other than faith in the government.

Iceland perhaps offers the best illustration of the huge risks taken and the long-term damage done. At the time, great mystery surrounded the way in which the Icelandic banks, based in a country with a population of just 400,000 people and highly dependent on the fishing industry, had managed to become a global financial force capable of financing takeovers all over the world. In the autumn of 2008 all was revealed when these banks, built on crumbling foundations supporting mountains of securitised debt, came crashing down. Before this happened, however, they had managed to wrest control of great chunks of

Britain's high streets – from the eponymous frozen food chain Iceland, to famous toy store Hamleys and the department store group House of Fraser.

The confusion and complexity of the markets was given a further stir by sloppy regulation, poor accounting and (in some cases) sheer deviousness that allowed banks and companies to park deals and financing off the balance sheet. The collapse of the Houston-based energy firm Enron in 2001 and the implosion a year later of the telecoms group Worldcom were instances of financial mismanagement on an epic scale, but although reform followed with the passage of America's Sarbanes-Oxley Act, which sought to clamp down on faulty accounting, loopholes remained.

Among the loopholes was the use of special purpose vehicles, off-balance-sheet entities, which allowed companies to hide the true size of their exposures to dodgy loans. In 2007–2008 such vehicles were to prove a material contributory factor in the credit crunch. Even now, companies in the financial sector – especially the banks – seem heavily attached to off-balance-sheet dealing. As was seen in 2008, behind the public face of finance was a shadow banking system comprising investment banks, such as America's Bear Stearns and Lehman Brothers, which enjoyed intimate relations with the hedge funds. These institutions acted as intermediaries between investors and borrowers, often having high levels of leverage that sustained a high ratio of debt relative to liquid assets.

Investment banks borrowed from investors in the short-term money markets. Eventually these loans would have to be repaid, requiring refinancing. The initial cash raised was lent to corporations to do deals on the stock market or invest in longer-term assets such as the securities created out of mortgages on people's homes. Relying on short-term borrowing for longer-term investments is a recipe for financial disaster for any financial group, as Northern Rock discovered. Many of the same mistakes made in the sub-prime mortgage market were repeated during the private equity and foreign takeover boom of the same period. Equally as startling, they would be a feature of the sovereign debt crisis in Greece and across the globe that would follow.

Cheap money, slack regulation, innovative financial products – all these factors allowed industrialised countries to become big borrowers and helped decide the future ownership of key British companies in a market that successive governments had been keen to keep as open as possible.

But there is one more important piece to the economic jigsaw: the unbalancing of the global economy. Put simply, the majority of Western economies ended up being driven by consumption and financed by debt, while those of the East ended up being driven by manufacturing and exports. In the process, the borrowers – known as the 'venal' countries and including the US and Britain – ran huge export deficits, while the lending – or 'virtuous' – countries saved and ran export surpluses, in the process becoming bankers to the rest of the world. These virtuous nations included Germany, China, Japan and South Korea and the energy-rich countries of the Middle East who conspired to keep the price of oil high.

In the short term, the fact that Asian and other exporters preferred to spend their surpluses in mature financial markets, rather than in under-capitalised emerging economies, helped stimulate the credit boom of 2003–2007 – described by Ben Bernanke, the thoughtful, gently spoken, bearded chairman of the Federal Reserve Board since 2006, as a period of a 'global savings glut'. In his 2010 Frankfurt speech 'Rebalancing the Global Recovery', Bernanke noted that these years witnessed large capital inflows into the US and other industrialised economies which – together with historically low interest rates – facilitated the creation of 'excess liquidity' in the global financial system. Bernanke traced events back to 1990 when emerging economies in Asia and Latin America became net importers of capital (in 1996, they borrowed $80 billion net on world capitals markets). These inflows were uncontrolled and not constrained by governance or fiscal discipline – hence the 1997 crisis which saw meltdown across the booming countries of East Asia from Thailand to Korea and Indonesia.

In seeking to rebuild their economies in the wake of the crises, Bernanke argued, these Asian countries 'increased reserves through the expedient of issuing debt to their citizens, thereby mobilizing domestic saving, and then using the proceeds to buy US Treasury securities and other assets'. Effectively, governments acted as financial intermediaries, channelling domestic saving away from local uses and into international capital markets. The economies of Asia were transformed from borrowers on global markets in 1997 to big lenders a few years later.

Major exporting nations sold their products to American and European consumers and then parked their surpluses – over and above their imports – in government securities. The Western banks became flush with cash and only too keen to lend. The investment houses, many of them owned by the big commercial banks, constantly dreamt up deals designed to utilise the easy credit. In multinational companies, private equity houses and ambitious individual investors they found clients ready to use the money to exploit their global ambitions. One way to achieve this was to buy companies and other assets overseas through takeovers.

The rise of China to become a mighty player in the global economy was central to the reshaping of the global financial landscape. In 2010 more than 70 per cent of America's gross domestic product (its national wealth) was based on consumer spending. For decades, the US funded its consumer boom by borrowing from its own citizens by issuing IOUs in the shape of Treasury bonds. Now foreign countries, and in particular China, became big buyers of US bonds. The Chinese largely manufacture the goods consumed by Americans and are paid with money they have lent.

Every month the US sells Treasury bonds to China so that Americans can buy more of its goods. Between 1996 and 2004 the US current account deficit increased by $650 billion – from 1.5 per cent to 5.8 per cent of GDP. Financing these deficits required America to borrow large sums from abroad, much of it from nations running trade surpluses, mainly the emerging economies in Asia and oil-exporting countries. Large and growing amounts of foreign funds flowed into the US to finance its imports.

By 2007 the US debt in the hands of foreign governments stood at 25 per cent of the total, compared with just 13 per cent in 1988. At the end of 2006, non-US citizens and institutions owned 44 per cent of federal debt – of which two-thirds sat in the central banks of other countries, most notably those of China and Japan.

The seemingly endless willingness of surplus countries such as China to lend to the US by buying its bonds enabled Alan Greenspan to keep interest rates low after 9/11. As a result, every month America falls deeper into debt while China accumulates more dollars. US indebtedness to China is greater than China's net deficit with all other countries. Much to the irritation of successive US governments the Chinese have also kept their exports cheap by keeping their currency – the Renminbi – artificially low.

China could have used its vast surpluses to build a social security system and encourage domestic consumption. Instead it has chosen to invest directly abroad not just or even principally within the OECD club of richer nations but in the developing world as well. In the developing world, its efforts have been spurred by a determination to secure the natural resources needed to underpin fast growth. When it comes to Western nations it is often design, research and development, technology and distribution that are its targets.

A good example of the Beijing approach occurred in 2004 when IBM, pioneer of personal computers, decided to throw in the towel and cede the market to its Chinese rival Lenovo in a deal valued at $1.25 billion. Having acquired the technology, the design and the distribution the new Chinese owner began to market itself as Lenovo across the globe while retaining some of the subsidiary branding such as 'Thinkpad'. Most Western buyers of PCs and laptops would not even recognise that they are now buying a totally Chinese product.

Closer to home, in 2005 two Chinese firms – the Shanghai Automotive Industry Corporation (SAIC) and Nanjing Automobile Corporation – made rival bids for control of the remnants of the UK's last mass market car group MG Rover. Rover had been placed in receivership following bankruptcy, and negotiations involved both the receiver and the UK government since local employment issues were raised. Earlier in the year, after a first failed attempt to take over Rover's assets, SAIC had bought the rights to sell two Rover models in China.

The common feature to each of the two bids was the relocation of Rover's manufacturing to China. Given that MG Rover was a failed enterprise, brought to its knees by its previous owners the Phoenix consortium and consigned to the scrapheap by the New Labour government, finding any buyers, let alone those that promised to keep some production in the UK, looked to be a face-saving formula. And true to the word of SAIC and Nanjing, 300 research and development engineers still work out of Longbridge, Birmingham along with a modest design and assembly team. But the pattern – Chinese ownership leading to the relocation of manufacturing – is a significant one.

China is not the only emerging market economy to have seen opportunities in Britain's industrial heritage. Indian investor Tata has swallowed Europe's biggest steel firm Corus as well as Jaguar Land Rover. Mexico now dominates our cement production following the 2005 acquisition of RMC (ReadyMix Cement) by CEMEX. Paradoxically, capital from emerging markets has been used to purchase a variety of prestige manufacturing enterprises at a time when through the World Bank and other aid institutions the UK is still providing foreign assistance to the very same nations.

Over the past decade, then, a variety of factors have come together to facilitate the foreign takeover of British concerns – and there is no sign of a slackening of pace. The question is: does it matter?

Many bankers and politicians would argue not. Economics commentator Will Hutton, by contrast, is one who thinks it does. Writing in the *Observer* in February 2006, he highlighted his concerns:

> Takeovers are not all one-way traffic: we buy companies in other countries. But no other economy is as open as ours with takeovers so easy. And, apart from the US, no other economy needs the inflow of overseas cash so acutely. Britain's industrial and financial jewels are being auctioned to pay for a record trade deficit . . . with no end to the deficit in sight, the auction will go on until the cupboard is bare.

Perhaps a hint of one of the potential pitfalls in this brave new world lies in a remark that Marcus Agius of Barclays made to me when we met in 2011:

> When I was an active merchant banker, and I don't see this in any sense to be embarrassed, I was like a mercenary. I felt very strongly that so long as a client was honest, so long as the client obeyed the rules and was respectable, my half of the bargain, in return for the fees, was that I served the best interests within the law as it stood.

A case can be made for a lack of sentimentality or sense of firmly rooted ownership in the world of finance. But when it comes to manufacturing businesses, to public services, to key utilities, should we be concerned that so many British companies have fallen – and continue to fall – under foreign control? That question barely impinged on the national consciousness until the US giant Kraft Foods came knocking on Cadbury's door.

3

The Battle of Bournville

Throughout the summer of 2009 the Cadbury World visitor centre at Bournville was in full swing and incredibly busy. Dedicated to the history of chocolate, it played host to thousands every week, guided tours of the massive factory culminating in visitors having the chance to buy well-known brands at discounted prices in the factory shop. Such favourites as Dairy Milk, Bournville, Milk Tray, Flake, Creme Eggs, Crunchie, Roses, Fudge, Picnic, Buttons, Curly Wurly, Wispa and Boost were all eagerly snapped up.

These famous product lines had made Cadbury a household name and a much-loved company. And it had certainly come a long way. Back in 1824 when it was established by John Cadbury it was no more than a grocer's shop in Bull Street, Birmingham. Cadbury, a Quaker, was opposed to alcohol and, like many teetotallers of the time, was anxious to promote the rival appeals of tea, coffee, cocoa and drinking chocolate.

Within seven years Cadbury had become a manufacturer, renting a warehouse close to his shop, where he began producing cocoa and chocolate. In the following decade his brother Benjamin joined and the company duly was renamed Cadbury Brothers of Birmingham. It received a much needed boost in the 1850s when the government reduced the high import taxes on cocoa, so bringing chocolate within reach of the masses. The firm grew and began renting a factory, and in 1854 the brothers opened an office in London and received a Royal Warrant as manufacturers of chocolate and cocoa to Queen Victoria. John's sons, Richard and George, later took over the business and launched Cadbury Cocoa Essence.

By now Cadbury had outgrown the Birmingham factory and began looking for land outside the city to build its new premises. A site was found four miles away and a 'factory in a garden' later named Bournville opened in 1879. To cope with a five-fold growth in the workforce more land was bought in 1894 and a village to house staff was built. The choice of the name Bournville – derived from Bournbrook – was a shrewd one: its Gallic ending evoked images of French chocolate, at that time regarded as the best in the world.

Anxious to compete effectively with Swiss and French chocolate manufacturers, the company constantly improved the quality of its products until it could finally claim that they were superior in quality and taste. It was at the forefront of new recipes and new ideas. It also became a major exporter, its first order from Australia arriving in 1881. At the turn of the twentieth century, the first milk chocolate bar rolled off the production line. At this stage, the company employed 2,500 workers at Bournville.

But Cadbury was no ordinary company. Far ahead of its time, the company provided workers with housing, education and training. Pension schemes and medical facilities ensured a healthy and dedicated workforce. George Cadbury, the idealistic son of the founder John, masterminded the move to Bournville and regarded employees as part of his family and treated them well and with recognition for their services.

'George wanted to create a utopia,' says Alan Shrimpton, of the

Bournville Village Trust (BVT), set up to look after the village. Caring for others remained an important part of the way the firm was run and today around eight out of ten employees have volunteered, or are volunteering, to help with charities and community projects, with staff allowed time off to organise fund-raising events.

By the early part of the twentieth century, Dairy Milk had become a household name. After the First World War the factory was redeveloped and mass production began in earnest. A merger with J. S. Fry and Sons in 1919 saw the integration of well-known brands such as Fry's Chocolate Cream and Fry's Turkish Delight – still sold today. In 1915 Milk Tray went into production and became a resounding success.

The firm opened its first overseas factory in Tasmania in 1921 and by 1930 Cadbury had become the 24th largest manufacturer in Britain. The romantically inspired Roses brand was launched in 1938 as Cadbury's products became market leaders. The company was now at the forefront of world chocolate manufacture.

During the war years, chocolate was regarded as an essential food and placed under government supervision. After 1945, however, normal production resumed and Cadbury went from strength to strength. More factories opened, new products were launched and improved technology enhanced production. The company's success brought about a merger with drinks firm Schweppes, which, too, became a global leader – buying the historic American brand Dr Pepper as well as an assortment of sports beverages.

Success continued into the new century. The company cut its debt and propelled sales growth through clever marketing, tapping into Britain's love of both chocolate and nostalgia with the relaunch of the Wispa chocolate bar, and devising strong campaigns such as the 'drumming gorilla' TV advertisement. It also increased its foreign holdings, buying the Adams gum company in America from Warner Lambert, a pharmaceutical firm, in 2003. The purchase helped to boost Cadbury's sales growth to 6 per cent a year. Cadbury applied some marketing pizzazz and innovation to the traditionally dull gum operation and gained access to the lucrative and fast-growing Latin America.

Cadbury's diverse nature, however, was seen by some as a weakness, and a number of shareholders pressed for change. They were led by the restless American activist-investor Nelson Peltz, a scourge of enterprises he considered to be performing below their best.

Under pressure from Peltz to deliver improved shareholder value Cadbury decided in 2008 to demerge its soft drinks arm Schweppes – owner of America's third biggest fizzy drinks brand Dr Pepper. The sale was achieved by a flotation on the New York Stock Exchange and released immediate returns for investors. It left behind a tidier confectionery business focusing on chocolate, gum and sweets. This offered huge growth potential – particularly in the newly wealthy markets of Asia and Latin America – and Cadbury, with its tradition of developing new brands, invested in expansion.

The stock markets, as sceptical as ever, remained unconvinced and, by late 2008, Cadbury shares were trading at less than £5 each and many of the big UK long-term shareholders had bailed out. Indeed, American 'value' investors showed more warmth than their British counterparts towards Cadbury and the demerger.

Nevertheless, despite the lack of investor recognition, Cadbury began 2009 in great shape. It was operating in more than 60 countries, including several fast-growing economies such as India and Brazil. It was also a supplier to the world's biggest supermarkets – Walmart, Costco, Tesco and Carrefour. Pre-tax profits for 2008 were £559 million – a 30 per cent rise on the year before, with earnings per share rising to 29.8 pence. At the start of 2009 anticipated growth for the year was estimated at 4 per cent and a confident Todd Stitzer, the company's Anglophile American chief executive – with a taste for handsomely tailored Savile Row suits – described the company as, if not 'recession proof', at least 'recession resilient'.

Cadbury's success inevitably also made it a takeover target, its attractiveness ironically increased by its earlier decision to dispose of its soft drinks arm. What had once seemed to potential predators to be something of a poison pill had now disappeared. What remained was a coherent and well-run giant. Global food enterprises eyed Cadbury's empire enviously, but no one went public with a declaration of intent.

All this changed in the summer of 2009 as food giant Kraft Foods started to plot a raid from its Chicago base that would revive memories among City veterans of the glory days of 1980s' corporate sharks.

One observer noted at the time that the bid came 'completely out of the blue'. Perhaps he should not have been surprised. After all, Kraft was a match for Cadbury. Stuffed full of big-name brands, it had become one of the world's largest food groups, second only to Nestlé. It also had a venerable history to match Cadbury's. Kraft itself began at the turn of the twentieth century, but technically its history can be traced back to the late eighteenth century when companies it has since acquired started in business. Among its more recent acquisitions were some of the most resonant names in chocolate. These included another emblematic British firm, Terry's of York founded in 1767, the Swiss chocolatier

Suchard founded in 1825, Tobler founded in 1867 and coffee roasters Maxwell House, which dated from 1892.

Kraft itself was launched in 1903 when, with $65 in capital, a rented wagon and a horse named Paddy, J. L. Kraft started purchasing cheese at Chicago's Water Street wholesale market and reselling it to local merchants. Within a short time, four of J. L. Kraft's brothers joined him in the business and, in 1909, they were incorporated as J. L. Kraft & Bros. Co.

Five years on, J. L. Kraft and his brothers purchased their first cheese factory in Stockton, Illinois. Within 12 months, they began producing processed cheese in tins. This method was so revolutionary that in 1916 Kraft obtained a patent for it and a year later the company started supplying cheese in tins to the US Government for the armed forces in the First World War.

The firm followed up on the brothers' success with processed cheese in tins by creating or acquiring many additional products. These included processed cheese in loaves, Velveeta processed cheese, Philadelphia cream cheese, Miracle Whip salad dressing, and Kraft Dinner Macaroni and Cheese. Innovative advertising was used to promote the products and Kraft was a pioneer in the sponsorship of television and radio shows. Kraft Music Hall on radio and Kraft Television Theatre helped prove the effectiveness of advertising on the then-new media. Aggressive sales merchandising techniques contributed further to the company's growing market share in an increasingly diverse line of products.

The success of J. L. Kraft and his company was drawn to the attention of Thomas McInnerney, founder of National Dairy Products Corporation. In 1930, it bought Kraft-Phenix Cheese Corporation, though Kraft continued to operate as an independent subsidiary.

Kraft's transformation from a successful American firm into the world's second largest food company came with its acquisition by tobacco corporation Philip Morris in 1988 for $12.9 billion – one of the largest non-oil takeovers in US history. With smoking increasingly unfashionable, world sales falling and expensive court cases to settle, Philip Morris knew that they needed to diversify quickly and radically. As Deborah Cadbury wrote in her 2010 book *Chocolate Wars*: 'The sheer scale of mergers that followed beggars belief.'

In 1989, General Foods linked up with Kraft. This was soon followed by mergers with Suchard, Tobler, and Terry's of York. In 2000, Philip Morris bought Nabisco, the maker of America's favourite Oreo cookies, for $19.2 billion, and merged it with Kraft. A year later Kraft Foods Inc. was listed on the New York Stock Exchange and early in 2007 Philip Morris (which by then had become the suitably anonymous Altria Group) voted to spin off the Kraft Foods shares and the company became fully independent of tobacco two months later.

That same month, the feisty Irene Rosenfeld became chairman. She was a force to be reckoned with. Born Irene Blecker in Brooklyn, New York in May 1953 to Jewish parents of European origin (her father's family was Romanian and her mother's German), she was a psychology graduate with an MBA and PhD in marketing and statistics who had begun her career in consumer research at advertising agency Dancer Fitzgerald Sample. In 1981 she went on to work for General Foods, which was bought by the tobacco group Philip Morris four years later. When Philip Morris bought Kraft in 1989 and merged the two, Rosenfeld moved from New York to Kraft's Chicago base. She rose to run Kraft in Canada and North America before leaving in 2004 – a decision many read as being motivated by her unhappiness with Kraft's owner, Altria Group (formerly Philip Morris). Her own comment was: 'Food and tobacco have different characteristics, and over time the food business was not able to make the investments that were needed.'

She took a year off to consider her options. 'It was the first time in 22 years I had ever stepped back and thought about what I wanted to do,' she has since recalled. Ultimately, though, sitting around doing nothing was not an option. She took over as chief executive and chairman at PepsiCo's Frito-Lay snacks operation and then returned to Kraft Foods.

She partly credits her success to being a parent (she has two daughters): 'This taught me a lot about being a better manager – parenting is one of the best management training programmes there is,' she once said. And she partly credits her success to her second husband, Richard Illgen, an investment banker, whom she married after her first husband Philip died in 1995. 'He made a critical decision almost 20 years ago to leave a large company and be self-employed because we were moving a lot and it was challenging. He has been terrifically supportive,' she explains.

In 2010 Rosenfeld's pay package, including new share awards, reached $19.2 million (£12 million), making her the 48th highest-paid boss on a list compiled by Forbes magazine. Although she eschews much of the personal trappings of wealth (her favourite gadget is an Apple iPhone), her two main corporate perks are the private jet – inherited from the previous management – and security for her £2 million home in the affluent district of Kenilworth on the shores of Lake Michigan, a short drive from Kraft's headquarters in the Chicago suburbs.

Away from work, she attends social events and is an active fund-raiser for local organisations – supporting Chicago's successful bid to stage the 2016 Olympics. But she doesn't seek the limelight and dislikes giving interviews – as is suggested by a trademark frown, and a degree of impatience. Those who know her speak of her as being 'polite but driven', of having an 'inner core of steel' and being 'very smart, decisive and clear thinking'. She is said to worry away at questions like a sparrow with a worm.

By the time she rejoined Kraft Foods as chief executive, she was a 25-year veteran of the food and beverage industry. A year later she took on the additional role of chairman. And she knew she had a challenge on her hands. Maxwell House coffee, Philadelphia cream cheese, Ritz crackers, Oscar Meyer frankfurters and Kraft cheese slices had been around for years and were seen as unexciting. In the parlance of the publicly quoted markets, Kraft had gone 'ex-growth'. It was Rosenfeld's job to restore the marketing pride and razzmatazz desired by the markets in branded goods companies. Kraft's long-term revenue expansion was just 4 per cent with earnings growth predicted at 7 to 9 per cent. With better earnings growth appearing to elude her, Rosenfeld was under pressure from shareholders to liven up its performance.

In 2007 she paid $7 billion for France-based Danone's crackers and biscuits business, turning Kraft Foods into Europe's largest cookie company. By 2009 it employed 98,000 people in 168 plants and generated annual sales of over £26 billion. Even with all this, however, growth was still a concern. Despite the company's phenomenal size and spread, many of its brands were in established Western developed markets, yielding low growth for investors.

It was in the context of these muted results that a concerned Kraft Foods board met in its sprawling headquarters at 3 Lakes Drive in Northfield, Illinois, one of America's largest corporate campuses. Rosenfeld had to find a way to push a sluggish Kraft forward. She needed to do something that would be a 'game changer' and believed that she had the answer: a sizeable purchase that would bring synergies and cost-cutting.

Cadbury was top of her wish-list. It was a success story. It seemed a good fit. There appeared to be an insatiable demand for its chocolate and other confectionery and chewing gum products. Possibly through a colonial legacy, Cadbury remained the leading chocolate brand in many fast-growing markets, including Australia, India, New Zealand, Malaysia and Singapore and throughout Africa. The confectionery business was valued at £10 billion with annual sales of £5 billion. Cadbury represented a major slice of this.

Rosenfeld calculated that adding Cadbury's products to Kraft's portfolio would increase annual revenue growth to 5 per cent and boost earnings by as much as 11 per cent. She was also attracted by Cadbury's shrewd distribution strategy: its products had a good position in 'instant consumption' channels, such as corner shops and petrol stations, where customers are prepared to pay higher prices when making impulse buys. By contrast, Kraft products concentrated on traditional spots, such as neighbourhood supermarkets, where margins were lower.

International growth was the clincher, though: 'It's all about growth' was Rosenfeld's mantra regarding the deal. Cadbury had annual sales of £240 million in India, where Kraft Foods barely existed, and £184 million in South Africa, where Kraft could only muster £50 million. Cadbury also had a useful presence in Mexico and Turkey where Kraft was relatively weak. The chance to get Kraft snacks into these emerging markets could be balanced by offering Cadbury the opportunity to get into Brazil and China where significant middle-class growth over the next decade was predicted.

There was another less tangible factor to be considered too. Kraft Foods suffered from an image problem among many in the food industry because it made most of its money from processed cheese and meat. A mass market confectioner, with a reputation for quality and creative marketing, would add lustre.

All in all, a coming together would offer 'the best of both', as Rosenfeld put it, creating a global powerhouse. Kraft operated in Britain, but only in a small way: it was home to its Irish operation with just 100 staff. Rosenfeld, though, believed she understood British conditions and, more importantly, the Cadbury culture. She would later say: 'We knew Cadbury was a British icon – that was one of the reasons we were interested in it – we value its heritage, and the passion for the brand. It matches the passion Americans have for Kraft brands . . .'

But Rosenfeld had to get it right. Simply adding Cadbury's chocolate output to the Kraft portfolio could be viewed by cynics as a clumsy bid for growth by bolt-on acquisition, a strategy that did not always deliver. Would a takeover bring real cost-cutting or the right synergies? Analysts calculated that Kraft would need upwards of £625 million in cost savings to justify the deal. Mergers and acquisitions specialists Glenboden went so far as to say that Kraft should concentrate on consolidation rather than diversification.

Rosenfeld, however, was determined to press ahead. Her key team, which included Tim McLevish, Chief Financial Officer, Marc Firestone, Corporate and Legal Affairs Chief, and Michael Osanloo, Strategy Chief, met to refine their plan, and by August 2009 they were ready to make their move.

Late in the afternoon of Friday the 21st, Cadbury's chairman, the rugged, veteran deal-maker Roger (later Sir Roger) Carr, who had recently escaped a turbulent stewardship at pubs group Mitchells & Butlers, found a voicemail on his mobile phone while waiting at Lisbon Airport. It was from Rosenfeld: she would be in Europe the following week and wanted a chat. As Carr later recalled, the message seemed 'innocuous'. The 62-year-old therefore arranged the meeting for the 28th in his Mayfair office at the Burlington Lane headquarters of the energy giant Centrica, where he was also chairman. Rosenfeld flew into London the night before and stayed at The Ritz Hotel on Piccadilly, just across the road from Carr's office.

Rosenfeld arrived at 9.30 a.m. dressed immaculately in her trademark dark two-piece suit. According to Deborah Cadbury, after exchanging pleasantries Rosenfeld told Carr: 'You know I have this great idea that we should buy you.' Over the next 20 minutes she unveiled a £10.2 billion cash-and-shares informal offer for Cadbury. In an interview with me Carr described Rosenfeld as 'clinical'.

Carr's response was abrupt: no deal. If Kraft wanted Cadbury the offer would need to be 'huge'. Unperturbed, the confident Rosenfeld explained that she would courier a formal letter of intent that afternoon and demanded a formal answer to her proposal by Wednesday. The meticulous Carr replied that the company would respond when it saw fit.

A flurry of phone calls followed. Carr rang Chief Executive Stitzer, the then non-executive directors including former Conservative minister and EU commissioner Lord Patten and Baroness Hogg, who chairs 3i, the private equity group. They were told that an emergency board meeting would be held on the following Monday – the August Bank Holiday – at the Fleet Street offices of the company's investment bankers Goldman Sachs. Carr also called Cadbury's trio of banking advisers: Simon Robey at Morgan Stanley, Karen Cook at Goldman and Nick Reid at UBS. The board meeting went on to endorse Carr's decision to refuse the offer.

Next, Stitzer, 57, a US-born corporate lawyer appointed chief executive in 2003 after two decades with the company, fulfilled a long-standing commitment. The snappily dressed naturalised Briton travelled to America for meetings with 40 of Cadbury's top shareholders. Unusually for a UK-based enterprise, American investors owned almost half of the shares. Despite all the patriotic fuss in Britain, the American investors were crucial to Cadbury's future. During those briefings, Stitzer learned that Rosenfeld's next move would be to go public and take Kraft's offer direct to the chocolate maker's shareholders: what is known in the business as a 'bear hug'.

Insiders at Kraft Foods explained that they had been patiently awaiting Cadbury's reply. But when it became clear that talks had reached a dead end, Kraft felt it had no option but to inform Cadbury shareholders directly of its plan. 'We wrote them a very nice letter. It was very gracious and polite. We even did proper British spellings,' joked Kraft's strategy director Michael Osanloo.

On 7 September, Kraft Foods announced to the London market the £10.2 billion or £7.45-a-share offer, which was swiftly rejected by Cadbury, even though the markets reacted positively and the company's value shot up. With the rising prospects of a takeover in cash, hedge funds and other short-term investors piled in hoping to make quick profits.

The possibility that Kraft might conquer Cadbury galvanised the chocolate world. The company's US cousins Hershey's – which made Cadbury products under licence in North America – hired investment bankers J. P. Morgan to examine its options. It had long been considered a possible merger partner for Cadbury, but Hershey's protective ownership by a Pennsylvania-controlled trust made a deal highly complex and very political. European rival Nestlé consulted its bankers Credit Suisse, while the secretive Italian confectionery group, Ferrero, famous for its

Ferrero Rocher hazelnut truffles, raised its head above the parapet. And the Qatari Investment Authority and Chinese and other Middle Eastern investors were all reported to be closeted with advisers.

The bid battle lines were now drawn and Cadbury's public relations machine roared into action. Much of the British press wanted Cadbury to wrap itself in the Union flag and appeal to the government for protection. As a global player, it had other ideas, probably best summed up by the quote from General George Patton printed on a placard in Stitzer's office: 'Nobody ever defended anything successfully, there is only attack and attack and attack some more.'

From the outbreak of hostilities in August, I had been struck by the degree of aggression shown by Cadbury: Carr went so far as to accuse Kraft of being an ex-growth busted flush seeking to buy into Cadbury's expansion story. It seemed to me that we were witnessing an Anglo-American reversal of roles: Britons – in the shape of Carr – appeared brash and aggressive. This contrasted with his Kraft counterparts' apparent reserve and more measured approach: they chose to portray themselves as preserving and developing brands and being very aware of ecological issues.

Cadbury, in other words, went in all guns blazing; Kraft took things more coolly. Trevor Datson, Cadbury's former head of global financial communications, recalled the mood. 'This was war. We unashamedly enlisted Cadbury's excellent reputation and levels of trust in the media to fight our cause.'

A 36-hour 'council of war' was convened by senior Cadbury people at Brocket Hall, the Hertfordshire stately home and golf club, where strategy was discussed and the defence team shaped. It was agreed that over the coming months Carr would be the public face of Cadbury, dealing with media interviews and negotiations.

Stitzer would concentrate on running the business and developing challenging growth targets which would make it more difficult for Kraft to execute the deal and ensure that if it did win it would be forced to pay a good price.

A formidable 'defence' team was assembled. It included City magic circle lawyers Slaughter and May, head of mergers and acquisitions Stephen Cooke and corporate partner Tim Boxell taking the lead. Since its key shareholding was based in the US, Cadbury also brought in long-standing American advisers Shearman & Sterling, led by Creighton Condon in London, to work alongside Slaughters.

Kraft Foods deployed one of London's leading law firms, Clifford Chance, to act as the main transactional advisers. US corporate partner Sarah Jones and her London counterpart Guy Norman headed the Clifford Chance team on the deal. Kraft also enlisted Gibson, Dunn & Crutcher to advise on US securities issues and Cravath, Swaine & Moore to assist with the financing of the deal. Arnold & Porter worked on US and EU competition aspects, led by London anti-trust partners Tim Frazer and Susan Hinchliffe. Other firms involved in a deal that would generate lavish fees included Cahill Gordon & Reindel, Herbert Smith and investment bankers Citigroup, Deutsche Bank and Lazards.

From the outset, Rosenfeld argued that the strategic rationale of a tie-up with Cadbury was 'undeniable' and would achieve $625 million of synergies and cost savings. The stock market was less convinced and Kraft's shares initially fell 6 per cent on news of the deal – usually a sure sign that investors are not convinced of success. But Rosenfeld was undeterred and the price steadily recovered despite Cadbury's public resistance.

Cadbury insisted that Kraft's offer was too low and many of its investors agreed that a 'big sweetener' was required. Legal &

General Investment Management, the biggest UK-based institutional shareholder, publicly declared that the Kraft offer undervalued the business. Analysts in the City predicted that to win the battle Kraft would have to raise its price to between £8.50 and £9.50 a share.

But as the *Economist* would later note, the rise in Cadbury's market value after Kraft's opening bid actually sealed Cadbury's fate. Over the whole course of the bid, nearly one-third of Cadbury shares would switch hands – most ending up in the hands of hedge funds and speculators – with the aim of cashing out with a quick profit. As Carr observed:

> People who owned 5 per cent suddenly owned more than 30 per cent and were looking to take a 20p turn on an £8 investment for three weeks. That was a 30 per cent return on their investments. So they were motivated by that opportunity.

The speed of change on the share register highlighted the declining interest of long-term investors in holding UK equities. Ultimately, 60 fund managers decided Cadbury's outcome.

From the outset, Stitzer received daily reports on the company's rapidly changing share register as trades took place at a blistering rate. North American investors, initially so crucial, dropped from 49 per cent to 27 per cent as funds cashed in. Meanwhile, short-term traders such as hedge funds went from holding 5 per cent (about average for a leading British company) to 31 per cent. Many investors had secured some profits by selling their Cadbury shares to the hedge funds in a process known as 'top slicing'. The sharks were circling and looking for a quick kill by gambling on the bid succeeding. In reality, the battle became a matter only of the price that the Cadbury board could squeeze out of Kraft Foods.

A month of hectic activity followed. On 22 September Cadbury stepped up the pressure by asking the City referee, the Takeover Panel, to impose a 'put up or shut up' deadline: in effect, it was asking Rosenfeld to show her hand. Eight days later the Panel gave Kraft until 9 November to make a formal bid. At the same time, Business Secretary Lord Mandelson – a self-confessed Cadbury's Fruit & Nut fan – waded into the issue, suggesting that foreign ownership of British companies could damage the country. This was something of a first for government ministers, who until the Cadbury bid had shown total indifference towards foreign takeovers.

The sometimes oleaginous Mandelson was rather different from some of his predecessors. He was a consummate politician who recognised the unpopularity of this bid among the public. It would not pass under the radar, as the loss of control of such companies as British Plaster Board and British Oxygen Company had done.

On 21 October Cadbury raised the stakes by upping its sales and profit margins, forecasting annual sales growth of around 5 per cent. It had become customary in takeover bids for incumbent managements to gild the lily on prospects to force the bidder to raise the price and to stiffen the sinews of those who wished to keep the target company independent. For good measure, it warned that it would lose its unique culture if it were swallowed by Kraft Foods. A company intricately woven into the fabric of the nation would become just another brand for a fast-moving consumer goods group.

Kraft met the 9 November deadline. It adopted a hostile approach, effectively making a direct bid to shareholders and so bypassing the Cadbury board's recommendation. It didn't, however, improve the terms being offered. Cadbury swiftly rejected the 'derisory' bid, which was now worth £9.8 billion – equivalent to

£7.17 a share – because Kraft's shares had continued to drop in value since August. A new row erupted when it was disclosed that the 83 per cent state-controlled Royal Bank of Scotland had joined the syndicate funding Kraft and was helping to finance the bid via a £630 million loan facility. It seemed to some as though British taxpayers' money was being used to fund an overseas bid that might be deleterious to the national interest.

Elsewhere, Ferrero Rocher and America's Hershey's emerged as potential 'white knight' joint bidders for Cadbury. Companies subjected to a bid often try to see off unwanted predators by reaching out to friendly firms as potential partners. As confectioners, with a strong family culture, both the Italian and American firms were seen as more likely to believe in and protect Cadbury than a conglomerate of Kraft's scale and diversity. The interest of the family firms, together with reports that Swiss-based Nestlé might launch a bid, sent Cadbury shares to their highest level in two months.

When I met Rosenfeld that month over breakfast, at the offices of her public relations advisers Brunswick in the elegant surrounds of London's Lincoln's Inn Fields, she and her colleagues seemed to have little sense of how the UK media worked and she was clearly taken aback by the extent to which the deal was being discussed in public.

'It is my understanding that this is a confidential process,' she told me. 'So I was rather surprised to be reading about it in the papers. It seemed a little bit early and a little bit unusual.' Some months later, by way of explaining her aloofness, she would only add: 'I said what I wanted to say – no more.'

During the course of the conversation, Rosenfeld also sought to offer some reassurance. Plans were afoot to close Cadbury's Bristol factory; Kraft, she told me, would aim to keep it going. Cadbury were committed to using 'fair trade'-certified ingredients from the developing world; Kraft understood this.

December saw no let up in the pace of events. Kraft posted a 180-page circular explaining its bid to shareholders. With the distribution of this document to investors the 60-day timetable that dictated how City takeovers play out was in force. On 14 December Cadbury launched its official defence to Kraft's bid, raising its financial targets again and promising shareholders higher dividends. Then, in what turned out to be a last-ditch attempt to avoid Kraft's clutches, Cadbury let it be known that it had taken the bold step of initiating informal talks with Hershey's about a friendly deal.

Hershey's and Cadbury already enjoyed a collaborative arrangement whereby each produced the other's products under licence in their respective domestic markets. Arguably, a merger would leave Cadbury more in control of its own destiny than if Kraft took it over. An insider told Reuters at the time: 'As Cadbury go through this process, they feel as though they want to have a management say in the organisation and I think that they perceive that one of the suitors is better than the other.'

There were compelling reasons why Hershey's should take the idea seriously. Foremost was the concern that it could end up being left behind in a new world of mega rivals, where American giant Mars Wrigley and Swiss champion Nestlé would be joined by a Kraft–Cadbury colossus. It also had a culture that in some ways was quite similar to Cadbury's: both were family-built companies with a history of charitable involvement in their communities.

Carr thought that if various issues could be resolved, a merger with Hershey's would be 'a wonderful outcome'. But these issues proved insuperable. Apart from anything else, Hershey's was struggling to decide whether to take the risk of bidding for a company more than twice its size. After a few weeks, momentum was lost and the talks came to nothing. Carr later described the outcome thus: 'Hershey was paralysed by internal conflicts of opinion.'

Both Cadbury and Kraft camps came up for air during the Christmas and New Year break, but 2010 saw a renewal of hostilities, during which pro-Cadbury campaigners organised a mass chocolate-eating event in Victoria Square, Birmingham. It was already clear, though, that for all the brave talk of the company's history and traditional values everything would ultimately come down to money. The deal was in the hands not of a nation of chocolate fanatics but of a long list of hedge funds, investment banks and pension funds that made up Cadbury's shareholders.

At this point Kraft was slightly on the back foot. It revealed that only 1.5 per cent of Cadbury shareholders had accepted its bid. Then came news that major shareholder Warren Buffett – the 'Sage of Omaha', whose Berkshire Hathaway group had a whopping 9.4 per cent stake in Kraft – was warning the company not to pay too much in cash and shares on the deal.

Rosenfeld ignored Buffett, impressing many observers in the process. 'There are not many who could go eyeball-to-eyeball with Buffett,' said Peter Langerman, head of Mutual Series, Cadbury's largest shareholder. 'I think it says something about her resolve.'

Throughout this period, Nelson Peltz remained uncharacteristically quiet. Deborah Cadbury called him 'the silent player driving this deal'.

Rosenfeld was moving closer to her goal and on 5 January Kraft bolstered its war chest by selling its frozen pizza arm to Nestlé for $3.7 billion. This not only added momentum to the company's offer, but also confirmed that Nestlé – which had until then kept its powder dry – would not be bidding for Cadbury.

Seven days later, Cadbury released its final defence document, attacking Kraft's management and revealing that it had beaten its own target for operating margins in 2009. Rosenfeld arrived in London ahead of bid deadline day – 19 January – amid fevered last-minute speculation that the Kraft offer might collapse and that Cadbury might escape. But with Hershey's out of the running, Cadbury was out of options and out of time.

From her suite at the Connaught Hotel in Mayfair, Rosenfeld rang Roger Carr at 7 p.m. on Sunday 17 January and arranged a meeting for the following morning in a private room at the exclusive Lanesborough Hotel at Hyde Park Corner. Rosenfeld asked Carr to back Kraft's final offer and make any takeover much smoother. Hearing that Kraft would up its offer to £8.30 a share, Carr is reported to have commented later: 'The minute she said that I knew we'd lost. I knew the business was sold in the real world.'

After a break in the negotiations on 18 January, Carr and Rosenfeld resumed talks at the Lanesborough, where the Kraft boss agreed to an improved offer of £8.40 with a 10p dividend once the offer had been unconditionally accepted. The pair then made their way to the Stratton Street offices of Lazards, Kraft's advisers, where they were joined by the Goldman Sachs team on behalf of Cadbury. By 9 p.m. the deal was done.

Carr believed he had done his job by 'securing tomorrow's price today', but was in no mood to celebrate and refused to take part in a staged PR photograph shaking Rosenfeld's hand. At 5 a.m. on 19 January he rang Sir Adrian Cadbury to tell him the news before he heard about it in the media. The final offer, valuing the company at £11.5 billion and made up of £5 billion in cash and the rest in Kraft shares, was put to the Cadbury board. Within a week, the white flag had been run up and Cadbury's board recommended the sale.

Carr announced: 'We believe the offer represents good value for Cadbury shareholders . . . and we will now work with the Kraft management to ensure the continued success and growth of the business.' The *Daily Telegraph* noted: 'In the City, Roger Carr is winning plaudits for securing a reasonably good price for his shareholders. In modern financial markets, that is what passes for victory.'

The fall-out at Cadbury was immediate. Within hours of the announcement, Carr, Stitzer and chief financial officer Andrew Bonfield all resigned. Stitzer left in April with an astonishing £40 million pay-off made up largely of share options built up over a long career in the company. Corporate affairs director Alex Cole left in March, followed by commercial director Geoff Whyte.

What is surprising about the whole Cadbury–Kraft battle is not that it should have caused such public interest and consternation at the time, but that it should have caused any at all. There was nothing unusual about the Kraft bid, nor about the elaborate negotiating footwork that followed, nor about the final outcome after the sale was agreed. Ultimately, as with any business transaction, it all came down to money.

Moreover, Cadbury could not exactly be described as a key national asset. When I spoke to Carr after the event, he pointed out that far more strategic operations – 'the airports, the seaports, the chemical industry or Pilkington [the glass company]' – had gone to foreign owners with scarcely a concern raised. Nor was overseas involvement in Britain's love affair with all things chocolate anything new. Earlier Nestlé had taken over Rowntree, dismembering the company in the process and moving Smarties production from York to Germany. Kraft itself had form. It had, after all, bought Terry's of York in 1993 and then, within a couple of years, shifted production of Terry's famous Chocolate Orange to Eastern Europe.

What's more, Cadbury wasn't even a particularly 'British' company by the time that Kraft Foods swallowed it up. It held a special place in the hearts of many people in Britain, but as Carr pointed out '. . . they loved it in an Enid Blyton way' with little or no understanding of what it really was:

> Everybody believed this was a much loved chocolate business and with family involvement. It was certainly none of those things. It had gone public 50 years ago; the family put it on the stock market because ironically they couldn't agree who wanted to keep, who wanted to sell, who wanted to take the money. No member of the family has worked in the business for a decade. Actually 80 per cent of the business was outside the United Kingdom. In the end the business sold more chewing gum than chocolate.

The company even had an American-born boss and a strong US investment base. At the time of Kraft's opening bid, 49 per cent of Cadbury's shares were in the hands of North American investors; British funds held only 28 per cent. Some 85 per cent of its employees were based overseas. The jobs of those in the UK were not automatically secure because the headquarters happened to be in Slough. Three years before the takeover battle began, Cadbury had announced, for example, that it intended to close the Somerdale factory near Bristol, home of the Wispa bar among other chocolate delights. To add insult to injury, the company simultaneously proposed to invest more than £100 million in new facilities in Poland.

As for the deal itself, in financial terms it ticked all the right boxes. The £11.3 billion price tag was a more than respectable one. Carr's responsibility was to achieve value for Cadbury shareholders and he did this by getting the offer raised to £8.50, worth another half a billion pounds to investors. Investors duly made a killing. The board could confidently argue that they had done the best deal they could. Asked in an interview if she thought that the British were hypocrites for waving the Union flag when Cadbury itself had bought overseas and been deserted by so many of Britain's own institutional investors, Rosenfeld replied emphatically, 'Yes.'

The fuss over Cadbury, then, was in many ways fired by emotion rather than logic. As a nation of sweet-eaters – Britons are the highest per capita consumers of chocolate in the world – Cadbury was a brand that touched almost everyone in the country. 'I think more than anything the engagement of the general public with a brand that they've known and loved from childhood gave it the sort of personal association for many, many people who in other circumstances would have no knowledge or interest in the ownership,' a reflective Roger Carr told me.

As City Editor of the *Daily Mail*, and opposing the deal, I personally took calls from members of the Cadbury family who were shocked by what was happening but felt powerless to do anything about it. The Cadburys rushed to the barricades. Felicity Loudon, a member of the Cadbury dynasty, spoke out against the possible sale, calling Kraft 'a plastic cheese company'. She gave a passionate interview to the BBC's *Today* programme proclaiming: 'Kraft won't understand the history and the quality of the company.'

Sir Dominic Cadbury, 69, who had retired in 2000 and was the last member of the family dynasty to sit on the company board, was also quick to condemn the outcome. 'There has to be something wrong with the fact that it was so easy to acquire the company,' he said. 'I think the long-term value of Cadbury has not been reflected. Personally, and from my family's point of view, I'm very sad that this has happened.'

It was this level of outrage that sparked off political concern. Politicians who had previously shown little interest in who owned what found that the place to be was on the front line. Then Secretary of State for Business, the politically savvy and commerce-friendly Lord (Peter) Mandelson demanded a review, and the Commons' Business, Innovation and Skills Committee opened a series of hearings. The tussle was still going on 21 months after the original bid had been unsheathed with the panel accusing Rosenfeld – who had failed to attend the hearings – of steering 'close to contempt of the House'.

And if Cadbury did not present the most compelling of arguments against foreign ownership, the whole affair has thrown up some important issues. The first goes to the heart of the way in which major mergers and acquisitions are funded in the twenty-first century. Much of the financing of the Kraft deal came from debt – an estimated £7 billion in all. This brought Kraft's total debt level to a reported £18 billion. Most companies as highly geared as this are vulnerable to downturns in the economy. Debt also inevitably makes companies take a short-term view, making decisions that might help tide things over to the next quarterly results but that might not be in the company's long-term strategic interest.

Nor is it unquestionably the case that mergers of the Kraft–Cadbury variety ultimately always stack up. A 1997 study by the Centre for International Business Studies by Meloria M. Meschi at London's South Bank University certainly suggests their benefits may be, at best, limited and short-term:

The bulk of the empirical evidence on the profitability of mergers and on the performance of the merging partners shows that mergers are usually unprofitable and the only group who stand to profit from merger are the shareholders of the acquired company.

Professor Susan Cartwright of the Manchester Business School has been similarly sceptical. In her 2002 study 'Why Mergers Fail and How to Prevent It', she acknowledges the huge rise in the number of mergers and acquisitions over recent decades, but concludes that 'at least half failed to meet financial expectations'. One factor, she argues, is the lack of 'cultural compatibility' – even in deals between US and British companies.

Some top business people feel the same way. Sir Philip Green, for example, the bluntly spoken Topshop tycoon – who in 2004 sought to buy Marks & Spencer – is a great sceptic about most takeovers:

> Any idiot with a cheque book can buy a business. The art is in buying one at the right price and knowing what you want to do with it. Easily said, too rarely done.

Certainly, damaging mistakes litter the landscape. The $350 billion AOL–Time Warner merger of 2000 is perhaps the classic example, in which an attempt to bring together the very different cultures of an internet service provider and a content colossus proved to be disastrous. Management, staff and business integration proved impossible because of the huge gulf of understanding and the deal embarrassingly had to be unscrambled. Closer to home the hurried takeover of HBOS by Lloyds TSB in the autumn of 2008, to create the Lloyds Banking Group, led to value destruction on a giant scale. Shares in Lloyds, traditionally a safe haven, were pulverised, tens of thousands of jobs lost and the company had to be bailed out by the British taxpayer.

And it's not as though Cadbury was a struggling company looking for a lifeline. Before Kraft Foods came along, the business had reshaped itself into a tightly focused enterprise with a keen eye on emerging markets from India to Latin America. It had taken risks in order to succeed. As Tony Bilsborough, who worked in Cadbury's communications, noted in 2009:

> We are still an aggressive forward-looking company but that does not mean to say we have lost sight of the ethos that has always underpinned the company. It is possible to be successful and community-minded at the same time.

When Cadbury was swallowed by Kraft it returned to its earlier manifestation, this time as part of a food conglomerate with literally hundreds of brands. It became almost impossible to track its revenues as its operations became part and parcel of other Kraft-owned chocolate and snack brands.

The Kraft deal also highlighted vividly how little control or influence a nation has over a foreign-owned company operating within its borders. At the time of the acquisition various undertakings were made – about employment levels (Cadbury employed 5,600 people across Britain and Ireland) and plant closures, Kraft promising, in the heat of the takeover battle, to keep open the Somerdale plant at Keynsham near Bristol. It was an undertaking quickly abandoned. Amoree Radford, a former Somerdale worker who led a 'Save Cadbury' campaign, summed up the feelings of most Cadbury workers: 'I believed Kraft totally,' she told the BBC. 'But they made a fool of me. They are utterly despicable.'

Kraft has been cagey as to what has happened to employment numbers in the UK after the takeover. Nevertheless, it's apparent that the closure of the Somerdale plant and the transfer of some production led to the direct loss of 400 jobs, and the indirect loss of others in the supply chain. One hundred and fifty skilled employees at the company's Uxbridge headquarters were made redundant in the immediate aftermath of the takeover. And in 2011 Kraft gave notice that a further 150 posts would go at Cadbury's historic Bournville factory in 2012.

This, of course, is scarcely surprising. When companies need to cut capacity they will tend to chop factories and operations far from home first. Ford, fighting for its life, was quick to decide in 2008–2009 that preserving operations in Detroit and the US was more important than hanging on to Jaguar Land Rover. In the same way, Renault shut its Belgian factory in the late 1990s, rather than close one in France. Peugeot, which had taken over the old Rootes-Chrysler operation in Ryton near Coventry, closed its British plant in 2006 with the loss of 2,300 jobs, shifting production of the same Peugeot 206 model to a plant north of Paris. As trade union leader Derek Simpson of Amicus said at the time: 'It is inconceivable that workers in France would be laid off on this scale. Weak labour laws are allowing British workers to be sacrificed at the expense of a weak labour market.'

When it came to Kraft's conduct, Westminster's Business, Innovation and Skills Committee, after conducting full hearings, could barely contain its outrage. In a report issued on 6 April 2010 it accused Kraft Foods of 'acting both irresponsibly and unwisely in making its original promise to keep the Somerdale factory open'. It suggested that the company was either 'incompetent' for thinking it could keep the plant open or more likely had engaged in a 'cynical ploy' to 'improve its public image' during the conduct of a hostile bid. 'Its actions have undoubtedly damaged its UK reputation and soured its relationship with Cadbury employees,' the report said.

Committee chairman Peter Luff said: 'The controversy surrounding the Kraft takeover of Cadbury has rightly opened a debate on how takeovers in the UK are conducted. That debate must continue, as a matter of urgency, in the next Parliament.' Even the normally measured UK Takeover Panel – the City referee for mergers – issued a rare public censure.

Having criticised Kraft, the Parliamentary Committee went on to set out a number of undertakings given by Kraft to the committee in respect of the future of Cadbury. These included continuing to manage Cadbury from within the UK and producing Dairy Milk in the UK. Kraft also agreed that there would be no further compulsory redundancies among manufacturing employees and no additional plant closures in the UK for the next two years. Cadbury's existing pension arrangements would be supported along with its Cocoa Partnership and use of fair trade ingredients.

Luff added: 'Kraft gave us a number of undertakings on the future of Cadbury, which we have put in the public domain. Kraft will have to deliver, in full, on these undertakings if it is to repair the damage caused to its reputation by the woeful handling of the closure of the Somerdale factory.'

The report concluded that the government must monitor compliance with these undertakings and by July the Conservative Liberal Democrat coalition had signalled its agreement with all points raised by the committee.

They were fine words and fine intentions. As times toughened, however, Kraft lost no time in squeezing as much income out of its new acquisition as quickly as possible so as to pay down debt and please its American shareholders. In March 2010, Cadbury staff were told that pay would be frozen for three years unless they agreed to opt out of the firm's expensive final-salary pension scheme. In May 2010, as the country was embroiled in one of the most closely fought election campaigns in a generation, Kraft announced it was closing its Cheltenham headquarters and relocating to Cadbury's Uxbridge and Bournville offices.

Kraft, in other words, was largely immune to criticism. Indeed the company displayed little interest in what British politicians had to say. The Kraft boss refused to appear before the committee, telling Bloomberg: 'Appearing before the panel was not the best use of my personal time.' She took a similarly laconic view of the UK media, too, saying, 'They're not always accurate.' Not that she was unaware of the anger many felt: she was overheard by economic journalists telling fellow members of the business elite at the Davos summit that she was scared to visit the spiritual home of Cadbury in Bournville because of the scale of the protests.

In its review of the Kraft ownership, released in May 2011, the Commons Select Committee could barely contain its frustration. Irene Rosenfeld was sharply admonished for her refusal to appear before Parliament to explain breaches of Britain's Takeover Code and her failure to honour commitments made during the course of the bid battle. 'Neither that refusal to attend, nor the manner of it, reflected well on Kraft,' the committee concluded.

This lack of control extends beyond employment and the day-to-day running of the company to such fundamental issues as the future of research and development and the role that such expertise plays in the shaping of UK plc. Cadbury may not have been a cutting-edge engineer like Rolls-Royce, the maker of aerospace engines, or have looked to have been at the forefront of innovation like Dyson. But its value to the country was, in its own way, just as important. Like Britain's other major food producer, the Anglo-Dutch group Unilever, it was a centre of excellence. It employed hundreds of food technologists testing and developing products not just for Cadbury but for the whole food manufacturing industry. After the takeover, there was nothing to prevent Kraft removing jobs and labs to the US or elsewhere in Europe, so denuding the cluster of science-based testing centres so important in the food supply chain. The only plus the Select Committee could muster was that, so far, Kraft was continuing to invest in 'recruitment and research' at Bournville. But with the company headquarters now outside the UK and Kraft ready to bundle up Cadbury operations with its other chocolate and confectionery subsidiaries, it is impossible to guarantee that the research and development commitment to Britain will be retained.

Marketing skills may have been lost too. Cadbury was a past master in this area, and had been able to adapt its talent to tap into the fast-growing emerging markets of India and Latin America. Now that everything was being handled from Zurich a question mark hung over Kraft's ability to read local cultural differences. All the Commons committee could do was express a vain hope that Kraft fulfil its 'oft-stated public commitment to Cadbury's brand heritage'.

The outcome to date has been mixed. Kraft's main contribution to strengthening Cadbury branding has been its late 2011 decision to invest £7 million in new technology at Bournville, imported from Switzerland, which uses a spring mechanism to ensure that 'Dairy Milk' is in an upright position in retail outlets. An ominous note was sounded, however, when in December 2011 Kraft revealed that having reviewed its UK and European chocolate manufacturing facilities, it had decided that it needed to find ways of 'improving productivity across the sites'. In practical terms those five vague words meant that 200 posts would be going at the Bournville factory in Birmingham in March 2012.

Kraft is in a position, then, to ignore politicians and public opinion, to go back on undertakings, to move research and development at will. It can also largely bypass British taxes. Cadbury's average annual tax contribution in Britain had been around £125 million a year. But with the company's announcement late in 2010 that control of Cadbury was to be moved to Kraft's European headquarters in Zurich, that bill could decrease by half or more. Kraft insisted the move was part of a group integration process. Jonathan Horrell, its Head of Corporate Affairs, said that all Kraft's European brands had been run from Zurich since 2006 and Cadbury would now be part of that system. But it's hard to believe that was the sole reason for the decision. The taxman has enough difficulty collecting the taxes of UK-based multinationals; the chances of making any impression on corporations notionally responsible to the Internal Revenue Service in Washington are very slight indeed.

And if that all sounds highly theoretical, it is worth bearing in mind what happened when high-street chain Alliance Boots was bought by the Italian pharmacy king Stefano Pessina and private equity barons KKR in 2007 for £12 billion. Soon after the takeover, Boots – founded and based in Nottingham for 161 years – moved its headquarters to Zug in Switzerland, a prim, rich city of 25,000 souls which sits about halfway between Lucerne and Zurich. Before the takeover, according to an investigation by my colleague Ben Laurance, Boots paid £89 million in tax in Britain in its final year as a quoted company on the stock market. Now that it pays its tax in Zug that figure has shrunk to just £9 million.

There are two reasons for this. First, to finance the deal the new owners borrowed £9 billion from various banks – a move that allowed them to offset interest on the debt against profits. Secondly, whereas the corporate rate tax in Britain is 28 per cent (although it is in the process of being reduced to 23 and then 22 per cent), the rate in Zug is a modest 15 per cent. It's scarcely surprising, then, that Boots' affairs should have moved to Switzerland. Nor is it surprising that Kraft should have adopted the same approach with Cadbury.

This erosion of the tax base in the UK has caused concern. As the volume of foreign takeovers reached its peak in 2006, just ahead of the credit crunch, the murmurings about the impact on government revenues began to pick up momentum. John Whiting of professional services firm PricewaterhouseCoopers, for example, commented, 'It is probably one of the factors in the attrition of the tax base.' Professor Steve Bond, of Nuffield College, Oxford, similarly has expressed a worry: 'As multinational firms account for a higher share of corporate activity, there is certainly a danger that more of the UK corporation tax base will be shifted to lower tax rate countries, partly as a result of high borrowing by UK subsidiaries of multinational firms.'

The numbers bear this out. According to official data from Her Majesty's Revenue and Customs, tax receipts from those parts of the economy most affected by overseas takeovers have either remained flat in recent years, so making an ever smaller relative contribution to the overall corporation tax take, or have actually declined. In the period 2005/6–2009/10 tax receipts from such sectors as engineering and chemical construction, for example, remained virtually flat; receipts from transport and communications slipped. The resulting shortfall has had to be met from elsewhere. This is in part the reason why there have been increases in personal taxation, national insurance and the raising of the VAT rate to 20 per cent.

Of course, it is not only foreign-controlled companies that are able to engineer a reduction in their tax liabilities. Domestic companies are guilty, too. Back in the 1980s Lord Hanson's eponymous Anglo-Saxon enterprise paid virtually no British tax, organising its affairs so that income was routed via Panama. In 2008 a number of UK-listed companies, including WPP, United Business Media and Shire pharmaceuticals, announced they were leaving Britain for Ireland, citing the tax system as their reason for going. WPP chief executive Sir Martin Sorrell said in February 2012 that he was prepared to return now that the coalition government was reducing corporation tax.

In the City of London exploiting tax loopholes is a way of life. Barclays found itself at the centre of a storm in 2008 when it was revealed that it employed a team of high-powered tax experts at its offices in Canary Wharf who were paid handsomely to find legal ways to avoid tax all over the world. The bank's activities were described by one critic as a 'tax-avoidance factory'. When put under pressure, Barclays – like many other institutions – threatened to fly the nest. Bob Diamond, who took over at Barclays in 2011, made it known that he would consider moving the bank's highly profitable investment banking arm Barclays Capital to New York should the sector become, as he saw it, over-regulated or over-taxed. HSBC's new chief executive Stuart Gulliver argued that if the UK tax on its global income were to exceed the profits it made from its British operations then shareholders would want it to consider a move back to its native Hong Kong.

Among the biggest critics of organised tax planning in opposition was former Shell economist and Lib Dem economic spokesman Vince Cable. The man who would become business secretary in the 2010 coalition government noted with some disdain:

> Normally a man who has made the study of the Taxes Act and the accounting legislation a priority above all other things in life would be looked upon with some surprise. But within structured capital markets these men are Masters of the Universe commanding multimillion-pound bonuses and publicly humiliating those of lesser knowledge. These men are not the types who will light up a party and tend only to be able to communicate through snorts and grunts whilst thumbing the pages of *Tolley's Yellow Tax Handbook*.

Nevertheless, it is undoubtedly the case that while many large multinationals of UK origin are keen to minimise their tax liabilities, they are nevertheless significant contributors to the national coffers. Research by the representative group TheCityUK shows that in 2010, for example, the financial services industry accounted for 10 per cent of the country's gross domestic product and 11 per cent of British tax receipts. By the same token, foreign-owned companies are in a much stronger position to avoid the UK tax authorities – and, of course, they feel little obligation to do otherwise. Companies falling under foreign ownership will always be tempted to ship their taxation base overseas – low-tax Switzerland is a popular destination, as is Ireland (where, for example, Google has its European headquarters). International transactions between different arms of multinationals account for more than 60 per cent of world trade. Even though tax authorities closely scrutinise the prices of cross-border deals within multinationals to ensure they comply with 'transfer pricing' regulations – designed to compare deals with those conducted on an arm's-length basis – companies often succeed in shifting profits to lower tax countries in this way.

Some lower tax countries have other incentives to offer, beyond competitive rates of corporation tax. It might be asked, for example, why Spain, a smaller and less prosperous country than the UK, was able to launch an armada of bids during the takeover boom: Telefonica's absorption of O2; Ferrovial's purchase of BAA; Santander's takeovers of Abbey, Alliance & Leicester and Bradford & Bingley; and Iberdrola's capture of Scottish Power. The answer is that Spain's companies are effectively incentivised to do so by the Spanish tax authority which allows firms to offset against tax 30 per cent of the goodwill cost of any foreign corporate purchase. As Tory shadow trade secretary Alan Duncan (a minister in the 2010 coalition government) noted: 'Free markets and international competition are good for British consumers . . . but this only works if we play by the same rules.'

If nothing else, the publicity surrounding the Kraft takeover did at least lead to some hand-wringing and a moment of introspection.

Within days of the takeover, Sir Roger Carr was demanding reform. In a hastily arranged speech at the Saïd Business School at Oxford – widely circulated to City editors and leading politicians – he argued for radical change. He suggested that the victory margin in UK takeover bids be raised from 50 per cent plus one share to 60 per cent and that anyone buying shares in a company during an offer period should have voting rights frozen until after the battle had ended. The latter move was intended to prevent short-term holders, like hedge funds, having a say in the fate of heritage enterprises like Cadbury.

It was a significant speech from someone who was to become president of Britain's leading business group, the CBI. To some extent his views echoed those of the Unite union. It had campaigned for legislation along these lines – known as 'Cadbury's Law' – and called on Labour to fight the impending May 2010 general election with this proposal firmly in its manifesto. Reformers sought changes to the Takeover Code and demanded an updated 'public interest test', under which governments could intervene in the national interest. This right had been scrapped by Gordon Brown and Tony Blair – by then enthusiasts for free markets and light-touch regulation – via the 2002 Enterprise Act.

Specific measures to deal with Kraft-type deals were on their way. In October 2010, new rules designed to make foreign takeovers of British companies more difficult were unveiled as part of the biggest shake-up in regulations governing mergers and acquisitions since their inception in the 1960s.

Under the proposals, hostile bidders would be forced to unveil plans for the target company, including possible factory closures and job losses. Sanctions could be imposed against firms breaching this code. Predators would have to disclose the effects of highly leveraged deals, where a bidder borrows heavily to fund a transaction that could impinge on the future competitiveness of the target.

Companies that pledged there would be no job losses after a deal went through would have to keep their word for a year or face penalties. The timetable for bids and deals was to be changed so as to prevent predators placing established firms under siege. Once a takeover negotiation was made public, the bidder would have to launch a formal takeover within a month, walk away or seek an exemption order from the panel. This was clarification of what the financial press had dubbed the 'put up or shut up' requirement.

The Panel on Takeovers and Mergers, the City watchdog, was determined to stamp out 'virtual bids', where a potential bidder makes an approach but spends many weeks or months prevaricating, destabilising the business it has in its sights. It also moved to abolish inducement payments, or break fees, whereby a bidder must pay its target a fee if it pulls out. It claimed that break fees could discourage rival bidders, or attract counter offers at a lower level than would otherwise be the case. The panel ruled in the autumn of 2011 that the use of 'break fees' would no longer be tolerated unless there are exceptional and justifiable circumstances. The change should work in favour of shareholders seeking a higher price for their stock by making rival bids easier to mount. It should also prevent boards from locking themselves into deals with buyers, whether at home or from overseas, which investors do not favour. These changes, however, went no further than addressing certain abuses. They did not consider the core issues that foreign takeovers involve.

Both at the time and in retrospect it was ironic that so much hand-wringing should have accompanied the takeover of a company such as Cadbury, which was no longer that British and which manufactured goods that were not cutting edge or strategically vital. But the issues raised by the sale were – and remain – significant ones nevertheless. And they acquire even more importance when one comes to consider some of the other – far more important – companies that have fallen to foreign ownership over the past few years.

4

ICI's Disappearing Act

In the spring of 2007 speculation about ICI, the emblematic British speciality chemicals group, was rife. For several months shares had been on the rise, and on 3 April had jumped 7.1 per cent in one frenetic day of trading. It was widely assumed that a takeover bid would be launched sooner or later, perhaps by the American Dow Chemical Company, perhaps by someone else.

Consequently, Peter Ellwood, the bespectacled, white-haired and softly spoken chairman of ICI was not exactly surprised when he found himself taking a phone call from Maarten van den Bergh, his opposite number at the Dutch group AkzoNobel. A veteran company with a historic connection to the Swedish chemist and inventor of dynamite Alfred Nobel, AkzoNobel was, like ICI, a global paints franchise. It was bound to be sniffing around.

Ellwood and ICI's chief executive John McAdam were prepared. The board on its own and with its advisers had been working through the numbers carefully. They had been seeking to identify what the company would be worth were all its plans for the next three to five years to come to fruition, distilling their calculations down to a share price. If a buyer were to come along and offer less than the price the board had in mind or the price itself, they would be shown the door. If, on the other hand, the buyer made an offer that involved a 'huge premium' then the board, in Ellwood's view, would be obliged to take it seriously.

In response to Maarten van den Bergh's request for a meeting, the ICI chairman invited him and the Dutch group's chief executive Hans Wijers over to London. The Dutch pair duly arrived and made a bid. 'We are not interested in that figure,' Ellwood told them. Under pressure from the Dutch pair to present the offer to the ICI board, Ellwood agreed, confident he knew how his fellow directors would react and therefore also confident that they would be able to give a formal answer the same day. Sure enough, he was able to relay the answer 'no' a few hours later.

A few weeks later on Monday 18 June 2007, after a weekend of intense press speculation, AkzoNobel announced that it would be offering 600 pence for each ICI share, placing a value of £7.2 billion on its quarry. ICI shares duly soared by 16 per cent in early trading amid hopes of a bidding war. But Ellwood and his board, who had first been advised of the likely bid on 6 June, were ready with their response. In a statement ICI declared: 'The board of ICI considered this proposal and unanimously rejected it on the grounds that it significantly undervalues ICI. The board is very confident in the group's strategy and strong growth prospects.'

Over the next few weeks things moved quickly. On 6 July 2007 AkzoNobel was told by the City Takeover Panel, the referee for mergers in the UK, that it must make a formal bid for ICI by 9 August or withdraw from the fray for at least six months. This was another instance of the use of the 'put up or shut up' rule, intended to ensure that companies under siege from predators weren't constantly distracted from day-to-day business.

After consultations with ICI's key investors Akzo was back again on 30 July 2007, this time increasing its offer to 650 pence a share.

It underlined its determination to press ahead with the transaction by announcing that it would pre-sell ICI's adhesives and electronic materials subsidiaries to the German firm Henkel for £2.7 billion. Once again the ICI board rejected the offer, in effect demanding a higher price.

This duly came on 6 August 2007, on the eve of the credit crunch, when AkzoNobel raised its offer to 670p or £8 billion, and secured the right to take a look at ICI's books. The deal was finally completed on 2 January 2008, after AkzoNobel had agreed to sell its Manchester-based Crown Paints subsidiary to satisfy the European Union Competition Commissioner.

The battle for ICI, fought against worsening conditions in financial markets, was a largely bloodless affair. It raised little emotion among shareholders and the public and was only of real interest to investors and people who followed the financial news.

Yet the irony is that the loss of ICI to foreign ownership was, arguably, far more significant than the disappearance of Cadbury into the jaws of Kraft Foods. This was, after all, a company that had played a key role in the development of UK scientific and industrial expertise over many decades. Fully aware of the company's illustrious past, Ellwood even went so far as to check that there would be no political fallout should ICI end up in foreign hands. As he later recalled to me in his offices at packaging group Rexam:

> I did float the idea, many, many months before we even had an offer, to the civil service whether anyone in the government or in the upper reaches of Whitehall had any kind of policy on protecting British companies. The answer came back: 'Absolutely not. We don't feel in any way that it's part of a government's job to protect ICI or anybody else

from a foreign takeover. We're interested in jobs but we're not interested in who owns the company.'

ICI had certainly come a long way since it had been created through an exchange of shareholdings among four giants of the UK chemicals industry – Brunner Mond, Nobel Industries, United Alkali Company and British Dyestuffs Corporation – in October 1926. The terms of the deal, drawn up on four sheets of Cunard-headed notepaper aboard a transatlantic liner, envisaged the creation of a national champion selling some 5,000 different product lines worldwide and with £100 million of assets. And both under its first chairman Sir Alfred Mond and in subsequent years it thrived.

When I started work as a financial journalist in the mid-1970s one of the first things I learned was that ICI was the bellwether of the London Stock Exchange. Its half-yearly and annual results and the dividend declaration would move the market, in much the same way as the results of Microsoft or Apple shape the mood four decades or so later. It achieved the zenith of its power and influence in the Thatcher years. Under the leadership of the extrovert John Harvey-Jones, profits reached £1 billion in 1984–1985. Harvey-Jones, who went on to be a TV star as a mentor to struggling companies, focused on making the best use of the group's research and development genius to create a company that offered thousands of different products, ranging from pharmaceuticals to paints to agrochemicals. It led the way in the commercial exploitation of polyurethanes – which alongside plastics and polythene had been developed in the ICI labs – into such products as cavity insulation for walls, refrigeration on ships and durable soles for shoes.

The company also diversified internationally, becoming the

biggest manufacturer of pain-combating drugs in the US. Under the leadership of Harvey-Jones's successor Sir Denys Henderson, it found itself earning the majority of its profits overseas – from the Americas to the Far East. Its headquarters on Millbank, just along the road from the Houses of Parliament, reflected the company's status as a kind of 'civil service of the industrial world'.

In 1991, ICI came under takeover siege from Lord Hanson and Lord White of the acquisitive cost-cutting transatlantic conglomerate Hanson. They saw it as a rich plum ready for the picking. What the two Thatcherite Lords failed to anticipate was the feisty resistance of Henderson and the willingness of ICI group's management to make a strategic move to see off a hostile bid. Under pressure from shareholders ICI announced that it would narrow its focus, creating a streamlined company that would be resistant to Hanson's slash and burn approach to acquisition.

Sir Tom McKillop, the compact, chippy and moustached Scottish scientist who joined ICI in the late 1960s, thinks this was an inevitable and correct response to the group's tendency to operate too centrally:

> Although ICI had a fantastic set of values . . . the mistake it made was it continued to run itself as a very integrated company with a large headquarters. I believe if ICI had operated differently, it could have continued to act almost as a holding company. Instead, a lot of time was spent inward-looking, focusing on the centre. It was a fundamental mistake ICI made.

ICI now narrowed its focus. Under the tutelage of Henderson, and his successor Sir Ronnie Hampel, ICI saw off the Hanson threat and focused on delivering value to its own shareholders, culminating in its 1993 decision to spin off its pharmaceuticals arm Zeneca (which in turn merged in 1999 with Swedish company Astra), a pioneer in the treatment of oncology, cardiovascular disease, respiratory problems and the central nervous system. McKillop, who went on to head Zeneca (followed by a disastrous period as chairman of Royal Bank of Scotland), argues that the split from ICI 'was like a great stone had been lifted off our backs'.

Among the discoveries to emerge from the original ICI–Zeneca labs were the first beta-blockers, which have saved countless lives around the world, as well as innovative malaria treatments. In post-ICI days, Zeneca continued to innovate. In 2000, its ground-breaking agrochemicals business, largely the product of work done in the ICI laboratories, was merged with similar businesses owned by Switzerland's Novartis to create Syngenta, a global business based in Basel. In a handful of years, then, the pharmaceutical element of ICI had become Anglo-Swedish, with much of the research and development taking place in Scandinavia, while the agrochemicals element – which had created herbicides like Touchdown and Surpass, insecticide Karate and fungicide Amistar – moved to Swiss ownership.

As for the remaining core of ICI, this was further transformed in 1997, when Chief Executive Charles Miller Smith – who had been brought in from consumer goods giant Unilever – splashed out £5 billion on buying the speciality chemicals businesses of his former company. It was a move welcomed by the markets, who boosted ICI's shares to more than £12 each by mid-1998. The arrival of former Guinness brewing chief executive Brendan O'Neill as chief operating officer that year was meant to put the finishing touches on the dawn of a new ICI – as smart and as shiny as its Dulux paint. No more dull talk of the ethylene price cycle, but plenty more talk of paints, food, flavours and fragrances.

It soon became clear, though, that not all was well. Miller Smith had paid top dollar for the businesses at the top of the cycle. 'It was a strategy-driven decision,' says Martin Adeney, vice president of public affairs at ICI during the 1990s. 'Charles Miller Smith was shaken by the enormous cyclicality he found when he joined. I think the company paid that much to pre-empt an auction and then became a distressed seller.' By the time that Miller Smith had moved up to become Chairman and the larger-than-life O'Neill took over as CEO of ICI in February 1999, cracks were beginning to show. The company's debt was bigger than its £3.8 billion market value at the time and its shares had collapsed from a high of £12.44 in May 1998 to £5.40. It was required to engage in a face-saving rights issue of shares to existing holders to strengthen the balance sheet.

There are conflicting views as to the wisdom of choices made by the ICI board in the years that preceded its ultimate takeover by AkzoNobel. A February 2008 article in *ICIS*, the chemical industry house magazine, takes a critical view, chronicling 'the demise of this once-great chemical company' and asking 'how mergers and acquisitions can go so wrong'. It argues that the problems began with the 1993 spin-off of the pharmaceutical and agrochemical divisions of Zeneca which had been the real 'crown jewels' of the company, suggesting that ICI was a victim of the stock market fashion for 'creating shareholder value by breaking up con-glomerates of unrelated businesses'. In ICI's case the truth was that the conglomerate structure – similar to that of German rivals like BASF – was its core strength particularly in research and development. 'BASF,' the article argues, 'has grown into a world-leading chemical company that has retained a diversified portfolio including many commodity chemicals.' The same could be said for the American kingpins including Dow Chemical and DuPont.

Former ICI senior executive Bob Walker told *ICIS* that ICI was right 'to exit commodity chemicals in the business environment post the two oil crises of the 70s and early 80s. The attempt to switch to higher added-value/knowledge-dependent specialities was correct.' But, he went on, instead of focusing on the company's strategic role, the board responded to shareholder pressure which in the end also led to the sale of the company overseas. 'My overall feeling, after a lifetime of work, is of huge frustration and regret that the collective efforts of so many capable and professional people should not have had a better outcome,' Walker observed.

Decisions made in the immediate lead-up to the AkzoNobel bid are also open to question. Over lunch at the Reform Club on Pall Mall in central London, former boss Sir Ronald Hampel was philosophical but saddened by events. 'I shall shed a tear at the disappearance of the ICI name,' he noted, acknowledging that management errors may have been made:

> Sins of omission are rarely apparent. With the benefit of hindsight what I would have done differently in 1993 when we spun off Zeneca is to put more money into ICI's balance sheet. We thought we had done enough by taking all the debt out. We underestimated the restructuring costs, in particular environmental clean-up and pensions. These became a burden around the necks of subsequent ICI management.

Nevertheless, whatever problems the slimmed-down ICI may have had in 2007, the fact remains that with its focus on speciality chemicals, dyestuffs and paints it was continuing to battle strongly for Britain in overseas markets. Its research and development labs, from which so many industrial and chemical products had emerged, were still going strong.

What determined ICI's fate that year, therefore, was not that it was a company on the ropes, looking for a saviour. Far from it. What made it vulnerable was an official lack of interest in what might happen to it, and a tight – arguably over-narrow – corporate focus on share price to the exclusion of all other considerations. In my conversations with Ellwood – a man of unimpeachable personal integrity – he was unrepentant about the board's decision to focus on price alone:

> As you know, when the company was formed in 1926, it was an iconic company. It had been a huge organisation employing well over 100,000 people. When I took the chair in 2004, we were employing just over 20,000 people. Was it a British company? Of course it was a British company but it was also, and we saw it very much like this, a truly global and international company. ICI operated in 40 countries, 87 per cent of the staff were outside the UK, a third of the sales are in North America, more than a quarter of the sales are in Asia. About one-third of the shares were owned by institutions and people outside the UK. One of the main businesses is actually headquartered in the UK and 80 per cent of the profits come from outside the UK and China is the fastest growing market for ICI.

Shareholders certainly gained from the deal, at least in the short term. But did UK plc? The answer is undoubtedly not. Leaving aside issues like tax revenues for the Exchequer, the fact is that the ICI–AkzoNobel deal did not turn out to be one of those great

Anglo-Dutch partnerships like Unilever, Reed Elsevier, Shell or Corus. The ICI integration, intended to save €642 million, was a far from painless process. Some 29 factories, including several in the UK, were closed, eliminating 3,500 jobs. In early 2009 AkzoNobel revealed that it had plunged into massive losses of €1.1 billion (£970 million), largely as a result of the ICI deal forcing it 'deeper and faster' as it sought to complete the restructuring. More job losses were projected and a pay freeze was imposed on the company's 500 top executives and most of the company's employees. Earnings from Dulux, the paint brand at the heart of ICI, plunged 41 per cent under the new owners as the company was hit by troubles in the housing market on both sides of the Atlantic.

The group continued to struggle in 2011. While revenues climbed 7 per cent to €15.7 billion, earnings fell to €541 million. How ICI fared amidst all this is impossible to discern.

But perhaps the most significant and worrying loss has been that of a guaranteed skills base. For decades, ICI's reputation – and its profits – were founded on its ability to develop new products and processes. AstraZeneca's existence as a world-leading pharmaceutical company is testimony to this. But once ownership moved abroad, there could be no guarantee that research and development would continue to be based in the UK. Indeed, as the new owners struggled to come to grips with the scale of the merged entity, they immediately began to jettison ICI assets. Within days of the merger ICI's adhesives and electronic materials activities, both with their own research capacity, were sold off to German competitor Henkel for €4 billion (£2.7 billion). The 2007 AkzoNobel annual report laid out the company's strategy in stark terms:

ICI Paints, integrated in AkzoNobel; Speciality Starches, intended for new ownership; Specialty Polymers, integrated into AkzoNobel; Electronic Materials, on sale to Henkel in 2008; Adhesives, on sale to Henkel in 2008.

As of 2011, some research and development still remained in the UK: there are research laboratories in Slough and Newcastle, and plans were announced to open two new labs to research fire protection and powder resin polymers. But there is no guarantee that all or any of these will remain, particularly if AkzoNobel sells off further parts of the company.

'We still have got huge R&D intellectual property in the UK ... the plc hasn't lost that innovative power really,' Sir Peter Ellwood says. That 'really', however, reflects the note of doubt that must always now be attached to the discussion of continuing innovation in the UK. And it is worth noting that after taking over ICI AkzoNobel's chief executive Hans Wijers – the Netherlands' former economy minister – immediately took steps to subordinate ICI's operations to those of its new Dutch owners.

It's the uncertain future of ICI's research and development capability in the UK that is worrying, and it is this that makes the sale of ICI to Dutch buyers more strategically significant in national terms than the sale of, say, Cadbury to Kraft Foods. The 2007–2008 financial crash and its aftermath have revealed all too starkly the weakness of an economy so heavily reliant on banking and services. Yet no attempt has been made to preserve the entrepreneurial flair that forged great companies like ICI.

It is telling in this respect that, in 2007, while investment in research and development in the UK increased among British-owned firms, it declined among foreign-owned firms. The following year, according to the Office of National Statistics, only

£3.4 billion of the £25.6 billion invested in research and development in the UK was funded by overseas enterprises, despite their massive presence here. It's a worrying state of affairs, particularly when one bears in mind that foreign corporations now control 39 per cent of UK patents. This compares unfavourably with the figure of 13.7 per cent that represents control of homegrown patents by non-native corporations in the rest of the EU, and with the similarly low percentages of 11.8 in the US and 3.7 in Japan.

The likely future of British-based research and development at Dutch-owned AkzoNobel contrasts markedly with that at British-owned Dyson. Dyson's success has stemmed from such everyday items as the bag-free, suction vacuum cleaner, bladeless fans for the home, powerful hand-dryers for washrooms, dog-grooming tools and dozens of variations of household appliances. It has conquered 30 per cent of the UK vacuum cleaning market and now sells to 52 countries worldwide. And it has remained firmly focused on research. As James Dyson notes:

> We are continuing to invest heavily in R&D and we have nearly doubled our staff in R&D in Malmesbury (Wiltshire). We are the second biggest filer of patents in the UK after Rolls-Royce. We plough 15 per cent of our turnover into R&D which is proportionately more than the big drug companies.

Consequently even when Dyson took the decision to move manufacturing to Malaysia and the Far East, research and development remained firmly based in the UK. The company attracted some criticism when it announced that it was no longer going to manufacture its products in the UK, but it's interesting to note that it now employs more people in Britain than when it was manufacturing here – some 2,000, in fact, of whom 700 are engineers. It also turns over more and pays more in taxes.

As someone keenly aware of Britain's engineering heritage, James Dyson has been determined that the 'brainpower' of his company stays in the UK even if manufacturing is overseas. He is evangelical about British manufacturing and in his report 'Ingenious Britain' – produced at the request of Prime Minister David Cameron in 2010 – he advocated creating a better environment for high-tech companies through bigger tax breaks.

It's noteworthy, though, that many of Dyson's engineers actually come from overseas – and that more than 70 per cent of the engineering and technology postgraduates in the UK are foreign students. Dyson finds it hard to find home-grown talent. And this raises another issue. What happens to the supplies of skilled researchers and engineers that the country does possess when centres of excellence cease to be British-based?

The answer has to be that they go elsewhere. Expertise is most powerful when it operates in clusters. The success of Silicon Valley, for example, partly lies in the fact that it is a magnet for those involved in software development. As new companies start up, they draw on people who already have the skills required, and then, as they grow, they draw in those who want to acquire them. By the same token, once the demand for skills declines, so the skills base dissipates.

Westland, Britain's last scale helicopter maker, offers a textbook case of this. In the Thatcher years, Westland found itself at the centre of a political storm over whether it was best rescued by America's Sikorsky or through a European alliance. The US route was taken and in 1988 ownership shifted to British engineering group GKN. Under GKN's tutelage, Westland returned to profit in the 1990s on the back of a series of Ministry of Defence contracts. In 2001 GKN merged Westland with Italy's Finmeccanica helicopter division.

No sooner was the deal done than the newly named AgustaWestland began shedding staff in Britain with 1,000 jobs going. Critics argued that British jobs were being sacrificed because it was easier and cheaper to lay off staff in the UK than in Italy. In 2004, GKN announced that it was selling its shares in Westland to Italian owner Finmeccanica for £1.06 billion in a deal which attracted little political attention despite the furore of the Thatcher years.

Since then, much of the core research and development and design in Britain has been shifted to Italy, leaving Yeovil – where Westland has long been based – as an assembly plant. So when in 2011 new AgustaWestland chief executive Bruno Spagnolini took the helm and emphasised the importance of 'next generation technologies' that would give rise to rotors, blades, engines, avionics and electric power transmission and distribution systems, Westland and the UK received barely a mention. The skills had gone. One of the former Westland sites, a disused airfield in Weston-super-Mare now, appropriately enough, houses the Helicopter Museum.

And, closer to Silicon Valley, one has to assume that California-based Hewlett-Packard's £7.1 billion takeover of British software group Autonomy in 2011 is not, as some have claimed, a great triumph for Silicon Fen, Cambridge's high-tech park, but a potential nail in the coffin of British software expertise. After all, Hewlett-Packard was not acting out of some sense of altruism when it made the bid, but out of a desire to gain skills it did not have but needed to possess if it was to reinvent itself for its largely American base of investors.

Shadow Business Secretary John Denham was quick off the mark from his opposition frontbench to criticise the Autonomy deal:

> The question we should be asking is why technology companies seem incapable of growing any bigger before they are taken out by an overseas acquirer . . . When the centre of gravity moves elsewhere, it will always be tempting to scale back a British subsidiary when times are hard.

It's scarcely surprising that the science departments in British universities should have suffered in recent years – a sure measure both of the value Britain places on innovation and of the lack of opportunity for British graduates in the domestic market. It was not until 2011 that, in response to the lack of jobs in the more popular arts and media sectors, thanks to the country's economic difficulties, the number of students tackling maths, physics and other sciences at 'advanced' level increased and that one or two universities – including Portsmouth – announced that they would be opening physics departments. That, however, has to be set against the fact that between 1994 and 2010, according to data from the Higher Education Policy Institution, the number of universities offering chemistry courses dropped from 83 to 66; those offering physics courses declined from 69 to 47; and those offering material sciences degrees fell from 10 to 6 (in the same period, the number of universities offering media studies degrees climbed from 37 to 111).

The record in engineering is particularly woeful. Data collected from a wide variety of sources by the London School of Economics shows that in the decade to 1997 Germany produced three to four times as many engineers each year as Britain. The employers' group, the CBI, found that between 2001 and 2006 the number of electrical engineering students declined by 45 per cent. And in May

2008 CBI director general Richard Lambert noted that three-quarters of the nation's engineering companies expected a shortfall in recruitment.

'More companies are having to recruit internationally to fill the gaps,' he noted. 'We are not only putting our established businesses in the UK at risk but it makes us less attractive to international companies looking to invest.'

The power of clusters of excellence is well demonstrated in one area where Britain has created a high level of expertise: telecoms. Orange, O2 and Vodafone are all British in origin. Indeed Vodafone is perhaps the premier example of a British company that has made it big overseas. Having consolidated its position in the UK market in the 1990s with a series of acquisitions, it then looked abroad for opportunities. Soon it had established networks as widespread as Australia, New Zealand, Fiji and the US (through cellphone provider Verizon Wireless, America's biggest mobile operator). In Japan it acquired the country's third largest mobile operator J-Phone (subsequently jettisoned in 2006) and in Ireland it acquired Eircell (subsequently rebranded as Vodafone Ireland).

Nor has Vodafone been beyond making hostile bids when required. The battle for Germany's Mannesmann in 2000 was hugely controversial locally – and the biggest hostile takeover ever completed in Germany. Famously, the architect of Vodafone's expansion strategy Chris Gent (later knighted) almost blew the Mannesmann deal when he was overheard mocking his German counterpart from the comfort of a hospitality box at the South Africa v England cricket Test match in Cape Town. Vodafone has also successfully pursued a series of 'Partner Networks' with countries throughout Europe and beyond, from Finland to Austria and from Malaysia to Sri Lanka. Its buying skill has been matched by its ability to innovate: it is undoubtedly one of the most impressive companies operating today.

Orange has slipped a little since it was sold to France Telecom in 2000, while O2, once part of British Telecom, was sold to Spain's Telefonica in 2006 for £18 billion. But it is interesting to note that in June 2011, on the recommendation of senior British executive Matthew Key, Telefonica announced that it would base its digital operation in London. This would involve bringing over the company's Skype-style service Jajah, the Spanish social network Tuenti and Latin American internet broadcaster Terra – a move that would lead to 2,500 jobs in the UK. Whether that would have happened if companies such as Vodafone had not made the UK a centre of excellence in telecommunications is a moot point.

A similar argument could be made about Nissan's recent decision to build a new car at its Sunderland plant. Among the world's richest industrialised countries, Britain is one of only a handful not to have a large-scale, domestically owned and controlled motoring industry. Fortunately, the expertise that it built up over the many decades when British car manufacturers operated still exists.

There are those who would argue that none of this matters, that in a global economy where a company happens to be domiciled is irrelevant. The distinguished engineer and industrialist Sir Alan Rudge, however, is just one influential figure who would disagree. The lanky, bespectacled former chairman of engineer WS Atkins spoke out eloquently against the UK's passive approach to overseas takeovers at a lively lunchtime seminar at the Westminster home of the think tank Civitas in November 2010:

Why does ownership matter? As those who have experienced corporate life will readily recognise, the key issues linked to ownership are those of basic control. Ownership inevitably affects strategy; investment; taxes and where they are paid; employment; procurement; group synergies; R&D; stock exchange listing; diversification and location of operations; choice of products and markets and prospects for senior management. The location and culture of controllers of the business are important and will, over time, and in various circumstances, have a fundamental impact on the future of the business.

Veteran *Evening Standard* commentator Anthony Hilton takes a similar view:

Apart from the massive loss of corporation tax revenue that usually follows a foreign takeover, the national interest is damaged in a host of other ways – by the loss of top jobs, the loss of high-end research and the fact that the loss of a local head office can rip the heart out of a local community. Take the company out of the town, and you destroy the town.

And Richard Lambert, CBI Director-General, speaking to *The Times* in March 2010 admitted: 'Something is lost when British companies pass into foreign ownership.'

Control is everything. The foreign takeovers involving AkzoNobel–ICI, Pilkington–Tokyo Glass, Linde–British Oxygen, high-tech Hewlett-Packard–Autonomy – to name just a few – necessarily mean that control passes elsewhere. And once control goes, then expertise and research and development all too easily follow. Because it doesn't happen automatically or straight away, there tends to be little fuss made at the time. But that doesn't make the danger any less real.

It's intriguing to speculate, for example, what might happen to a firm such as Dyson if it was bought by a foreign competitor, such as Siemens of Germany (something that could, of course, only happen with the acquiescence of the founder and family of the company, since it is privately owned). It's possible that Siemens would choose to repatriate manufacturing, currently focused in the Far East, to Germany, where there is a strong supply chain for domestic appliance companies including Siemens itself and the even more upmarket brand of Miele. That wouldn't affect the status quo in Britain since Dyson already manufacture abroad. But what would be the prospects for the brains of the company in Wiltshire? Dyson is immensely profitable – it earned £206 million in 2011 – and a sensible buyer from overseas would clearly be anxious not to destroy the creative engineering culture. On the other hand, Siemens might think it made more sense to unify Dyson's intellectual property with its own. Given that even Dyson finds it difficult to recruit qualified engineers in Britain, and that Germany's universities and colleges are stuffed with engineering graduates, it would certainly make sense.

Doubtless there would be some grumbles from MPs, and a few despairing articles in the press, but since Dyson no longer manufactures in the UK, the general level of protest would be muted. In the meantime, a crucial centre of excellence would have left the UK, never to return.

It's notable how different the attitude of British governments – and, in particular, of the last Labour government – has been to that adopted by other countries. A number, such as France, Spain, Germany and the US, all have different forms of 'economic patriotism' in place, which make foreign bids for local companies difficult to achieve.

Take France, for example. There, widespread state holdings in vital utilities act as a brake on inward deals. The French have consistently resisted pressure to allow foreign energy companies to compete freely in their domestic market. They argue that it is in the national interest to prevent key technologies falling into foreign hands.

The policy is backed up by a published list of industries, including defence, which it shields from foreign takeovers. Among the ten sectors are several surprises, including casinos. In 2005 when it was reported that US drinks giant PepsiCo was poised to bid for food firm Danone, President Jacques Chirac declared that the French yoghurt-maker was considered a 'strategic' company and beyond the reach of foreign predators.

The French authorities also routinely interfere with commercial deals. In 2008, the merger of Suez and Gaz de France was engineered as a means of pre-empting a rival bid for Suez from the Italian energy group Enel. Two years later in August 2010 Suez took control of British generator International Power.

Spain has worked hard to ensure that the country's energy companies remain Spanish – for example, thwarting the 2006 bid by German energy group E.ON for Endesa. A year later Spain's Iberdrola bought Scottish Power. Nationally registered companies are allowed to write off goodwill against tax when making foreign acquisitions – in effect a state subsidy offering an advantage in any bidding war. When British Airways was able finally to merge with Spanish rival Iberia to create the world's third largest carrier, it was on the condition that board meetings would be held in Spain.

Germany – a country where private equity companies leading the overseas takeover revolution have been described as 'locusts' – is similarly resistant to foreign involvement. In fact, Vodafone's conquest of Mannesmann in April 2000 is one of the few hostile deals ever to have been completed on German soil. When, in 2011, aerospace group Rolls-Royce made a bid for seagoing engine maker Tognum, it was canny enough to make sure that it included Germany's Daimler in the takeover consortium to sweeten the pill.

Germany's caution extends to enterprises seeking to establish even just a foothold. Concern was voiced in 2007 when Dubai International Financial Center bought a 2.2 per cent stake in Deutsche Bank, the country's largest bank, and in 2010 when the Russians sought to win a stake in Deutsche Telecom. Berlin's response to such activity has been to pass a law that allows the government to veto foreign investment of 25 per cent or more in a company if such a venture is deemed to be a national security threat.

Elsewhere in Europe, the Swiss have kept Nestlé safe from prowlers. Among the BRIC economies China and Russia back their own brands in a display of what Business Secretary Vince Cable has described as 'authoritarian, nationalistic capitalism'. And while India has bought UK enterprises like Jaguar Rover, it has not reciprocated the favour by allowing British firms to take majority control in the country's financial sector.

As for the US, the country which likes to portray itself as a 'champion' of free trade is very far from adopting a laissez-faire approach in its own backyard – as Barack Obama's move to help the American car industry in 2008–2009 graphically demonstrated. Foreigners are, for example, not allowed to buy US airlines – overseas shareholders are only allowed to own 25 per cent of an American carrier. Television networks are similarly protected, which is one reason why the Australian Rupert Murdoch took on American citizenship. Oil is also jealously guarded: China's state-owned oil company was prevented from purchasing the struggling oil firm Unocal in 2005. When the more acceptable BP went astray over the Gulf of Mexico spillage disaster in 2010, it was exposed to the full force of hostile American nationalism. This came just four years after the takeover of P&O by Dubai Ports World from the United Arab Emirates had to be delayed and fundamentally restructured in the face of opposition from Congress because six east coast ports were included in the sale. Then CBI president Sir John Sunderland, formerly of Cadbury, criticised the move: 'Countries which should know better,' he stated, 'proclaim to believe in free trade, but when the competition knocks on the door . . . they always act to protect a "special case".'

America's neighbour Canada is also worth considering in this light. It has long lived in fear of US colonialism and has shown a relentless devotion to maintaining an independent culture and business climate. In recent times, post the global financial crisis of 2007–2009 – when Canada came out relatively unscathed – it has exhibited a new tendency towards economic patriotism.

In the summer of 2010, the London-quoted mining giant BHP Billiton, with interests spread across the southern hemisphere, launched a bid for Saskatchewan-based fertiliser group Potash Corporation. Once regarded as a deeply unfashionable industry, potash mining had become enormously valuable in the boom years before the credit crunch as China grew in prosperity and its demand for fertilisers like potash increased to meet the requirement of a population seeking a richer diet.

In the wake of the $39 billion bid, the state of Saskatchewan put enormous pressure on the government in Ottawa to block the transaction despite its financial attraction to investors. In November 2010, the bid was abandoned after Tony Clement, industry minister in the Conservative-led government, formally ruled it out:

At this time, I am not satisfied that the proposed transaction is likely to be of net benefit to Canada as required by Ottawa's foreign investment law . . . Canada has a long-standing reputation for welcoming foreign investment. The government of Canada remains committed to maintaining an open climate for investment.

A disappointed BHP responded that it had been unable to convince the government of the deal's merits despite 'unparalleled' pledges on jobs and investment.

Economic patriotism reared its head again in 2011 when the London Stock Exchange proposed a merger with its Toronto counterpart the TMX, arguing that together they would represent a powerhouse of natural resources stocks. Shareholders in the TMX rejected the London merger amid intense pressure from an Ontario citizens group.

As former chairman of Cadbury Sir Roger Carr summarised it in 2011 as the newly elected president of the CBI:

In France, the loss of a 'Cadbury' would be out of the question. Germany believes that strength at home is the first step to success abroad. In Japan, selling a company over the heads of management is unthinkable. And in the United States, regulations exist to protect strategic assets.

Given the suspicion shown by so many of Britain's competitors to overseas takeovers, why has Britain itself been so relaxed? Part of the reason lies in the country's love affair with banking and services, which from the late 1980s onwards have been seen as some sort of universal economic panacea. And, stemming from that, part of the reason lies in the fact that so many of the financial institutions based in the UK make much of their money from buying and selling companies. To seek to protect manufacturing in the UK is like trying to guard chickens in a coop to which the local foxes have been invited.

Yet it is apparent that the economic model arrived at in the 1980s and 1990s is now not enough. Britain may have become a financial powerhouse – with all the risk that proved to entail – but in the process it lost its taste for ownership of assets, and is suffering as a result.

In modern times, recovery from recession has always been export-driven. The 'NICE' decade followed the debacle which saw Britain expelled from the exchange rate mechanism, a sharp devaluation of the pound and an export boom. Success came on the back of failure, thanks to the strength of manufacturing exports. Perhaps not surprisingly, therefore, when, in the wake of the 2007–2009 financial crisis, the pound fell by more than 20 per cent against a basket of currencies of Britain's major trading partners, many experts, including the governor of the Bank of England, Sir Mervyn King, expected a similar export-led recovery.

Unfortunately, in the Tony Blair years in Downing Street, from 1997 to 2007, the share of the economy made up by manufacturing shrank from 20 per cent to 12.4 per cent. At the time, the loss of capacity was disguised by the financial boom. But once the economy crashed it became apparent that manufacturing was too denuded – thanks in part to overseas takeovers – to deliver an export bounce. By contrast, in Germany, where manufacturing represents 29 per cent of GDP and the supply chain is much stronger, output quickly recovered to pre-recession levels on the back of strong exports.

The contribution a major industry can make to a nation's economic welfare – and economic recovery – is nicely displayed by a company such as pharmaceutical giant GlaxoSmithKline (GSK).

Based in Brentford – with its spectacular glass headquarters beside the M4 motorway on the route in from Heathrow – it is the world's third largest pharmaceutical company measured by revenue, behind two American behemoths Johnson & Johnson and Pfizer. The company, with a vast global research and development network, has a rich portfolio of products for major disease areas including asthma, cancer, virus control, infections, mental health, diabetes and digestive conditions.

For the average British consumer it is probably better known for its consumer health care brands which range from Lucozade and the toothpaste Sensodyne to the indigestion formula Gaviscon, as well as a vast range of over-the-counter medicines.

The company started to expand globally in the late 1960s, buying seven laboratories in Canada and the US in 1969. In 1982, it bought Allergan, a manufacturer of eye and skincare products. In 1995, Glaxo spent £9 billion on a merger with the commercial arm of Wellcome.

This set the stage for the game-changing takeover of Philadelphia-based SmithKline Beecham in January 2000 in a share swap which created a group with a combined market value of $177 billion and worldwide sales of $25 billion. The deal, pioneered by Sir Richard Sykes of Glaxo and SmithKline's boss, the former tennis star Jan Leschly, was seen as necessary to give GSK the research and development and marketing strength to take on the American giants.

'We can honestly say we have a real powerhouse of a new company,' Leschly said at the time. Inevitably like many big mergers the Glaxo–SmithKline deal took years to settle down, but under the stewardship of Jean-Pierre Garnier, in the early years of the decade, GSK continued to build its bank of expertise, developing vaccinations for everything from cervical cancer to bird flu. Garnier's youthful successor Andrew Witty, who took over in May 2008, has continued the global focus but taken the group in a different direction. It acts more like a pharma finance house acquiring stakes in state of the art biomedical companies in California and around the globe.

Today GSK employs 16,000 people in the UK (its total workforce worldwide stands at 98,000). It is Britain's biggest spender on research and development, investing a total of $7 billion (£4.4 billion) annually, an increasing proportion of which is being spent in the UK (as a result of a favourable new tax regime confirmed in Chancellor of the Exchequer George Osborne's 2010 budget). Some 94 per cent of GSK's annual turnover of £27.4 billion is earned internationally, boosting Britain's exports and income flow.

Unfortunately, success story though GSK is, it is also something of an exception. Apart from defence, which is to some extent ring-fenced, the strategic heart of British industry has been weakened as one major manufacturer after another has disappeared. Steel-making was compromised with the sale of Corus to Indian conglomerate Tata in 2007. ICI was sold off. Engineering was undermined when Tomkins agreed to a £2.9 billion takeover deal by a Canadian consortium of private equity firm Onex Corporation and the Canada Pension Plan Investment Board. Glass makers Pilkington went, as did battery and industrial power pack maker Chloride.

Pilkington's is a particularly tragic loss. Founded in 1826 and based in St Helens, Lancashire, it prospered as an independent quoted company and became a major global player. It was a pioneer, too, perfecting the technique of float glass to produce sheets of uniform thickness and flatness, ideal for architectural work.

As the business became global so did ownership. After several previous failed attempts, the Japanese rival Nippon Glass offered £2.2 billion in 2006 and a reluctant board capitulated.

Such losses make economic recovery that much harder. And in the longer term they denude the country of entrepreneurship and expertise – and financial health.

5

Brands for Sale

Political indifference to foreign takeovers has tended to mask their sheer scale. The figures, however, speak for themselves. The Office of National Statistics reported that in 2009 British companies bought around £22 billions-worth of overseas companies while foreign business acquired £30 billion of British operations. A year later, according to data collected by information group Thomson Reuters, the gap had widened: British firms invested $38.8 billion (£24 billion) in buying firms overseas, while foreign companies spent $86.8 billion or £54.5 billion purchasing UK corporations. Even at the height of the takeover boom in the first decade of the twenty-first century, British firms spent on average only half the amount on acquisition that foreign companies were spending in Britain.

Foreign ownership extends to many businesses that have been traditionally regarded as quintessentially British. Consider the high street, for example. High-street chemist Boots, which began life in 1849 in Nottingham, has been owned since 2006 by Italian tycoon Stefano Pessina and US private equity firm KKR. A year earlier, the late Anita Roddick's Body Shop natural products chain, with stores around the country, was sold off to France's L'Oréal. Selfridges, with its chain of high-end department stores, which began life in

1909, was acquired in 2003 by Canada's Galen Weston for £598 million.

The same is true of some of the grander brands. Throughout its history, Harrods, the world-famous high-end department store on a five-acre site in Knightsbridge, has only had five owners – yet the last two have been foreign. In 1984, the Egyptian Al-Fayed brothers purchased a 30 per cent stake in House of Fraser, which owned Harrods, from 'Tiny' Rowland, the head of Lonrho. In 1985, the Al-Fayeds bought the remaining 70 per cent for £615 million, a move that sparked a long-running and vicious feud with Rowland who had also been seeking to buy Harrods. In May 2010, Mohamed Al-Fayed sold the store to Qatar Holdings for £1.5 billion.

Fortnum & Mason, with its Piccadilly headquarters and royal patronage, was founded as a grocery store – for which it has an international reputation for specialist high-quality foods. The store has since broadened its range to offer other goods and services. In 2001 it was acquired by Wittington Investments, a holding company for Weston family interests.

Harvey Nichols, founded in 1813, is another upmarket department store chain offering many of the world's most expensive brands in womenswear, menswear, accessories, beauty and food. In 1991, the store was acquired by Dickson Concepts, an international retailer and distributor of branded luxury goods based in Hong Kong. After a public listing in Asia and London the company returned to the private ownership of Dr Dickson Poon in 2003.

A similar pattern emerges with leading hotels. The Grosvenor House was originally one of the largest private houses on London's exclusive Park Lane area of Mayfair and home to the Dukes of Westminster for more than a century, before being demolished to make way for a luxury hotel. It now belongs to the American chain, JW Marriott. Similarly, the Dorchester, another luxury hotel on Park Lane which first opened its doors in 1931, is now owned by the Dorchester Collection, which in turn is owned by the Brunei Investment Agency (BIA), an arm of the Ministry of Finance of Brunei. The Dorchester Collection owns luxury hotels in the UK, the US, France and Italy. And the Savoy, built by impresario Richard D'Oyly Carte and opened in 1889 on its present site in the Strand, is now managed by Canada's Fairmont Hotels and Resorts, operator of luxury hotels and resorts in 16 countries. The Savoy remains one of London's most prestigious and opulent hotels after reopening in October 2010 following a three-year £220 million refurbishment.

British industry offers the same relentless pattern. I have already mentioned ICI's purchase by AkzoNobel in 2007. A few months earlier, in June 2006, UK glass manufacturer Pilkington was bought out by Japan's Nippon Sheet Glass. A few months after that, in January 2007, steelmaker Corus – the core of which was the old British Steel – was bought out by Indian conglomerate Tata.

Corus's fate demonstrates just how turbulent foreign ownership can be. The company was the product of various mergers over the years, culminating in the October 1999 merger of British Steel and Dutch firm Koninklijke Hoogovens. The Anglo-Dutch company had been the sixth largest steelmaker in the world and the second biggest in Europe, churning out 20 million tonnes of steel a year with annual revenues of £12 billion. It had factories at Port Talbot, Scunthorpe and Teesside, as well as steel processing operations in other parts of the UK. A total of 24,000 of its 42,000 staff worldwide were based in Britain.

Tata's £6.08-a-share bid saw off Brazilian rival CSN, prompting owner Ratan Tata to pronounce it 'a moment of great fulfilment for all in India – the first step in showing that Indian industry can step outside its shores into an international marketplace as a global player'. However, it was not long before the high price paid for an asset at the top of the market led to trouble for the company purchasing it.

As the recession really started to bite in 2009, Corus, owned by Tata, quickly moved to slim down its operations. Of 3,500 jobs axed worldwide, some 2,500 were cut in the UK – mostly in depressed regions hugely reliant on heavy industry. Some 600 jobs went at Llanwern, as part of a total of 1,100 cuts across the firm's Welsh operations. A further 1,400 jobs went at other UK sites, including 713 in Rotherham, where a plant making engineering steel employs 1,350 people and is the town's biggest private-sector employer.

That was not all. In 2010, Corus announced that it would be curtailing production at the 150-year-old Redcar plant in the depressed north-east putting 1,700 jobs at risk. New Labour, which had not raised an eyebrow when Corus had been sold to the Indian firm, was quick to make excuses for the closure. 'The steel industry has suffered an unprecedented fall in demand in the global recession,' Business Secretary Lord Mandelson argued.

A reprieve came in early 2011 when the Thai company Sahaviriya Steel Industries (SSI) revealed it had bought the plant from Corus for £300 million and would be able to re-employ 800 of the plant's former staff. It announced that it would use the plant to produce slab steel for the Far East. Arguably, similar ingenuity could have been deployed by a British-owned company producing a vital material in admittedly difficult times. But when the initial sale had taken place, discussions were centred purely on price, not on strategy.

This short-term approach invariably undervalues a company's

importance to its original host country – in terms of jobs, skills and expertise. It also underrates what a brand, which may have been built up over many years, may be worth.

This is apparent even in such a trouble-strewn area as the car industry. It is not a sector in which Britain has proved successful – today, along with Canada, the UK is the only country among the G7 richest industrial nations not to have a home-owned car industry. Yet, over the years, the country has given rise to an extraordinary number of famous brands, from Land Rover to Mini to Rolls-Royce. All these have struggled at various times, and when they have ended up falling into foreign hands there has been a general sigh of relief. One might compare, for example, the disastrous turn of events in 2000 when, with the backing of the Blair government, Rover was briefly taken over by the British Phoenix consortium, who proceeded to bleed it dry, with the relative security it was given when it was taken over by a Chinese state-owned company in 2005.

The point here, though, is not so much Britain's ability or inability to sustain its own car manufacturing as the value that other nations clearly place on classic car brands. The Mini is a very telling example. Forty-two years after it first saw the light of day, the classic Alec Issigonis-designed car was reborn, thanks to its new owner BMW. Today, some 100,000 Minis are produced each year at BMW's new factory in Oxford, with between a fifth and a quarter of them destined for UK car buyers. BMW calculated that the new Mini – seen very much as a nippy, hip motor for the young and image-conscious – would sell well despite its relatively high price. Sales proved them right.

The German ownership of Mini demonstrates the endurance of a strong brand – and the importance of long-term investment in good production values. BMW saved the Mini and created valuable jobs at the Hams Hall plant, where the engines are assembled. Arguably, a far-sighted British owner might have been able to achieve the same outcome. After all, there is still some automotive expertise in the UK, particularly in the high-spec, high-technology design that has spun out of Formula One motor racing. UK-owned firms like Surrey-based McLaren and Northampton-based Cosworth lead the world in high performance design.

In many ways BMW's aggressive marketing of the Rolls brand, among Asia's new rich, provides a graphic example of what can be done if domestic brands are carefully invested, nurtured and marketed. Burberry, still British-owned, demonstrates how a staid raincoat maker – with a focus on UK quality, manufacture and design – has been able to conquer the world as a luxury goods emblem. It has created an image for itself that gives a competitive edge in a fiercely cut-throat market.

Brands certainly survive – and can thrive under – foreign ownership. As Tim Leunig of the London School of Economics points out:

> Sometimes branding can survive a foreign takeover very well. People don't think of KitKat as a Swiss product, although it's owned by Nestlé, and I don't think they see Vauxhall as American. Sewing machine maker Singer is American, but widely perceived in France to be French. McDonald's restaurants in Britain are locally franchise-owned but perceived to be American.

But it's the very fact that great brands are so resilient and clearly so valuable to others that should make people think twice before they part with them.

English football has proven a perhaps surprising battleground for names that have acquired international recognition. The number of clubs that have passed into foreign ownership is extraordinary: indeed almost any club is now easy pickings for foreign poachers. Around half the Premier League clubs are, or have been, foreign-owned: among them are Aston Villa (American Randy Lerner), Blackburn (India's Venkey's Group) and Birmingham City (Hong Kong-based Carson Yeung), relegated in 2011. Overseas-dominated boardrooms can also be found throughout the English and Scottish professional game.

In some cases, the foreign owners who have swept in to buy up clubs have done so almost as hobbies, or at least as trophies. This trend stretches back to 2003 when Chelsea was bought by Russian billionaire Roman Abramovich. Since then the Russian oligarch has pumped £740 million of interest-free loans into the club, bringing them three Premier League trophies, a hatful of FA Cup triumphs and several appearances in the final stages of the UEFA Champions League, including the final in Moscow in 2008.

In a similar spirit, Abu Dhabi's Sheikh Mansour bin Zayed Al Nahyan – one of the world's wealthiest individuals – bought Manchester City in the summer of 2008. Since then he has sunk £750 million into the club, making it the sixth richest in Britain and among the top 20 in the world.

In part what may have driven such owners to purchase English clubs is the difficulty inherent in buying clubs on the continent. In Spain, Barcelona is technically a co-operative owned by the club's supporters. Real Madrid, meanwhile, is the property of the municipality which helps it renew its playing staff through land deals. The best-known Italian clubs are under control of the country's wealthiest families, with the media tycoon and former Prime Minister Silvio Berlusconi owner of seven times Champions League winners AC Milan. Big German clubs like Bayer

Leverkusen tend to be fiercely protected by local big business – in the shape of the chemical and pharmaceuticals concern Bayer – and the local municipality. And so on. English clubs enjoy no such protection.

Leaving aside the Abramovichs of this world, several of the overseas individuals who have swept in to take over English clubs have done so not to indulge a passion so much as to run – and profit from – a business. Manchester United is the obvious example here. Its owner Malcolm Glazer, along with his family, sees sports franchises as a commercial enterprise exactly like any other, and that is why they chose to take control of the Premier League club in May 2005.

United had become one of the biggest names in football. A great history and tradition allied to success had turned them into a highly influential, massively supported and very wealthy club. What's more they had a following far beyond British shores and their brand had not only become widely recognised but was highly lucrative.

The idea behind the Manchester United brand has been simple: consumer association with sporting prowess and success. The team wins and the fans buy into it not just through match tickets and TV subscriptions, but through the purchase of football kits and other merchandising. In the words of the consumer experts: United is a lifestyle brand – at their rarified level it stops being about football and becomes more like celebrity worship.

By 2005, United had become one of Britain's leading brands in a world largely dominated by the US. (An Interbrand survey at the time rated 42 of the world's top 75 brands as American, with just eight (or 11 per cent) being British – no great surprise, given that so many UK brands were being lost.) It was also susceptible to takeover since it had ceased to be owned by its original dynasty of

Catholic families and was a publicly quoted company on the London Stock Exchange. The biggest stakes were held by the super-wealthy Irish racing tycoons J. P. McManus and John Magnier who had been drawn into the club by its inspirational manager Sir Alex Ferguson.

But the Irish shareholders, with a 28.7 per cent stake in the club, fell into dispute with Ferguson over the ownership of classic and Group One thoroughbred racehorse Rock of Gibraltar, which ran in United's red colours.

The Glazers, meanwhile, had bought into United bit by bit, starting with a 2.9 per cent stake in 2003. They were finally ready to pounce in 2005 with a debt-laden, highly leveraged £790 million offer. The approach when it came was typical of an era of free-and-easy credit when the lenders expected to be paid back from future income of the asset. In the Glazers' case, part of the purchase was satisfied by payment in kind (PIK) loans where the interest charges were simply added to the loan.

The Glazers' buyout caused great concern among fans and the wider football community about the size of the debt – nearly £1 billion – that the club, whose parent company is Red Football, had been saddled with. However, it was not only the perilous financing structure that evoked hostility. The new owners were counting on an aggressive commerciality – still alien to Premiership soccer – to bring rich rewards.

They believed, rightly as it happened, that a combination of corporate sponsorship, TV rights and merchandising would offer huge international earning potential. The fear among the club's supporters was that the debt burden would inhibit the manager's ability to buy top players and, even worse, force the sale of prize performers such as the England star Wayne Rooney.

Remarkably, despite such rickety ownership, Ferguson – a

veteran Scot famed in the media for his terseness – was able to steer the club to the Champions League title in 2008 and its 19th Premiership title three years later.

Such accomplishments do not just happen. Behind the forbidding media image, Ferguson is a footballing genius. On social occasions he is both courteous and engaging with a catholic range of interest from contemporary politics to the American Civil War. The Glazers may not have been the favourites of the fans sitting at Old Trafford's famed Stretford End, but Ferguson found working with them congenial because, as he told one source over lunch, 'they leave me alone'.

Despite accumulating huge debt and the additional pressure brought about by the global financial crisis and recession, the Glazers were still firmly in charge of the club in 2011 when the first moves towards an Initial Public Offering – which would help the family repay its debt – were made on the Singapore stock market. After its interlude in American ownership, Manchester United was following the obsession with branding and fame all the way to the fast-growing Asia-Pacific region.

Undoubtedly, the Glazers' understanding of global branding and investment infrastructure at Old Trafford added long-term value to the franchise. It's a shame, though, that this understanding had to come from abroad. It's also a shame that so many of the financial rewards stemming from its improved cash flow and profitability should be destined to end up in the pockets of its American owners and new shareholders in the Far East.

It also has to be admitted that foreign ownership of English football clubs can cause tension with fans who feel that a club's owners don't always feel the need to take account of their views. In October 2011, for instance, Chelsea's ruling oligarch Abramovich found himself at loggerheads with a large group of supporters over the issue of a potential decision to move from Chelsea's traditional ground, located close to the King's Road and the most valuable piece of football real estate in Britain with a potential development value of well over £1 billion.

By contrast – and in a very different sphere – Tesco has graphically demonstrated how a great brand can be built, sustained and profited from. Having reached saturation point in the UK, where it controlled some 30 per cent of the grocery market, the company turned its attention overseas. It chose to grow organically, setting out its stall from Eastern Europe to Thailand, Japan and China. In America it has sought to establish the Fresh & Easy convenience brand across the western states. Former Chief Executive Sir Terry Leahy set the company the goal of producing 50 per cent of its income from overseas. By the time he left the group in 2010 it was well on its way, with his successor Phil Clarke, an old China hand, very focused on the Far East and global online opportunities.

The Tesco story is certainly an encouraging one. The company moved from a family-controlled 'pile it high, sell it cheap' model to multinational giant in just a few short decades, becoming the world's third largest retailer in the world measured by revenues behind Walmart and Carrefour. It may have suffered a wobble in market share and sales in 2011, but it remains a powerhouse, helped greatly by its new-found international reach. It has now established stores in 14 countries across Asia, Europe and North America and is the grocery market leader in Malaysia, the Republic of Ireland and Thailand. It has also demonstrated a sensitivity to local concerns in the countries where it operates by entering into joint ventures with local partners, such as Samsung Group in South Korea (Samsung Tesco Homeplus), and Charoen Pokphand in Thailand (Tesco Lotus), appointing a very high proportion of local personnel to management positions.

It also makes small acquisitions as part of its strategy – in South Korea, Poland and Japan in 2005–2006, for example (though the Japanese experiment was abandoned in 2011). By late 2004 the floor space Tesco operated abroad surpassed the amount it had in its home market for the first time, even though Britain still accounted for more than 75 per cent of group revenue.

Part of what has made Tesco so resilient is its keen interest in, and knowledge of, property. Just as it built a huge land bank in the UK – giving it the jump over rivals when it came to building superstores – it has done much the same overseas. In 2010, it revealed that in China it would be pioneering the concept of Tesco malls – shopping centres built around Tesco but joined by other retail groups. Its willingness to commit funds to overseas investment, on which the returns would be slow to arrive, set it apart from other UK scale retailers. And its relentless drive has taken a brand, known previously only in the UK, onto the international stage. That brand is now a very valuable asset.

One of the few key British brands to have resisted takeover to date is, ironically, one of the brands that has made so many other takeovers possible: the London Stock Exchange. With its 350-year history, and its reputation as the City's most important financial institution, it has certainly not been short of wooers.

In December 2005, it rejected a £1.6 billion takeover offer from Australia's Macquarie Bank. It then received an unsolicited approach from the American NASDAQ exchange which valued the company at £2.4 billion. After its bid was rejected, NASDAQ later gained a large stake designed to force new negotiations. Other potential buyers, including Germany's Deutsche Borse and Sweden's OMX, were also seen off.

In 2007, former chief executive Dame Clara Furse sought to place the LSE's fate in its own hands by forging a merger with Borsa Italiana, creating the London Stock Exchange Group. NASDAQ sold the majority of its shares to Borse Dubai, leaving the United Arab Emirates-based exchange with 28 per cent. In what was seen as a move to allow the LSE to retain its independence, Qatar also grabbed a 20 per cent stake.

So far, the LSE has managed to hold off its predators, although NASDAQ's interest may have been rekindled by the 2011 proposed merger between the New York Stock Exchange and Frankfurt's Deutsche Borse – the deal that was blocked by the European Commission in 2012. The fate of the LSE is essentially in the hands of Gulf countries, with Qatar also owning a 20 per cent stake. It is fortunate to have had, in the shape of Furse, a fiery, bouffant-haired Canadian-born financier, someone who was prepared to defend it. Not many other key British brands have been able to find such champions.

6

Home Services,
Overseas Ownership

Overseas ownership of football clubs, department stores, luxury car makers, thoroughbred racehorses and hotels might seem of only passing interest to many observers. After all, in a nation that courts the international super-rich from the Gulf potentates to Russian oligarchs and Greek ship owners escaping the trials of Athens, these are the everyday accoutrements that come with billionaire status. Overseas ownership of engineering companies, glass makers and other manufacturers goes similarly unnoticed: these organisations may be the engine house of an economy but for many they lack glamour and their ultimate ownership is a matter of only the vaguest interest.

But people feel very differently about their public services.

Every person in the developed world feels that it is their right to expect that when the switch is clicked down the power comes on, when the tap is turned water flows, that the airports operate efficiently and the elderly, whether in care homes or at home, are treated with respect. They assume that there will be sufficient investment in the services, a guarantee that regulation works and an assurance that public interest is weighed against profit motive.

The fact is, however, that when essential services fall into foreign hands, as has increasingly been the case in Britain in recent decades, it becomes harder to ensure that the interest of the greater good of the state and the welfare of the consumer top the list of priorities.

Thinker, broadcaster and writer Will Hutton, a senior figure at the think tank the Work Foundation, writing in the *Observer* in February 2006, noted that Britain was being sold off at a rate unprecedented in modern times. 'With this rate of takeover,' he remarked, 'within a generation, most British workers outside the public sector will be working for foreign companies. The scale of what is happening is breathtaking.'

Whether this was a matter for celebration or concern was a moot point. Certainly, in this pre-credit crisis era there were few people in the business world to question what was going on, as I found out to my cost when I attended the CBI's 2006 conference in Islington. I was there to deliver the case against foreign owner-ship. I swiftly realised, though, that I was on a hiding to nothing, particularly given that the panel ranged against me included Andy Bond, chief executive of the supermarket group Asda (owned by the American retail behemoth Walmart) and Jean-Louis Beffa, chief executive of the building materials group Saint-Gobain, which had recently bought British Plaster Board, a world leader in its field. Few if any others were willing to consider the risks involved.

Even the director-general of the CBI, Richard Lambert, was muted on the subject of foreign takeovers. A former editor of the *Financial Times* with a winning politeness and charm and a forensic mind, he was prepared to acknowledge the changing nature of business in Britain but not willing, it seemed, to explore the possible repercussions:

A wall of new money, facing curbs in other big European economies, has come crashing on to our shores in the past few years, in the process changing the ownership and national identity of a large number of UK household names.

It wasn't only business people who seemed sanguine about what was going on. Politicians, too, clearly regarded foreign takeovers as part of the natural order of things, and viewed those of us who questioned what was happening as old-fashioned nationalists and xenophobes who were out of touch with the reality of the modern globalised economy and who therefore failed to understand that ownership is unimportant.

Meanwhile, foreign ownership continued to expand. Treasury analysis, included in a report in the *Financial Times* on 25 June 2007, showed that in the ten years from 1997 (the Blair years) foreign ownership of British companies rose from 30 per cent to 50 per cent. What's more, an astonishingly wide range of sectors were affected – everything from motor manufacturing to investment banking and from retail to aggregates.

Among all these, it was those deeply embedded in the country's infrastructure that seemed to have been the most affected. In the boom years of the 1990s right up to the credit crunch of 2007 and beyond, nearly 40 per cent of companies involved in providing the population with electricity, gas, water, roads, bridges, rail, airports, ports and other key facilities acquired some degree of a foreign accent. By 2010, according to an Office of Fair Trading report, 20 per cent of the nation's vital services were owned by shareholders in foreign public limited companies; 28 per cent by UK public limited companies; 10 per cent by infrastructure funds under the control of various owners; 3 per cent by sovereign wealth funds (by their very nature overseas-controlled) and 19 per cent by public institutions. The balance of ownership was held by pension funds, private equity, banks and individual investors, many of which were controlled from overseas.

Foreign ownership was in the ascendency, and if the share of public services controlled by foreign public limited companies, sovereign wealth funds and infrastructure funds (several of which, like Macquarie, hailed from overseas) are added together then it can be argued that overseas owners dominate the UK's infrastructure. Moreover, it's not just physical infrastructure such as ports and power generation that have moved to foreign ownership; other areas, including care for the elderly, have been similarly affected.

The most extreme – and the most public – example of a vital service gone abroad and then gone sour has to be the residential health provider Southern Cross, which came crashing down in spring 2011. The company, which received most of its income from local authorities, had been pieced together between 2004 and 2006 by the hard-headed American private equity firm Blackstone, headed by billionaire Stephen Schwarzman, before being sold back to the public through a flotation immediately before the credit markets dried up.

Blackstone saw a commercial opportunity in buying up and stitching together privately run care homes across the country, creating a single entity which could source services centrally and provide a common standard of care. In some cases Blackstone also saw a property opportunity that involved buying up the freeholds and placing them in a separate investment vehicle. It believed that care homes, with a guaranteed regular source of income from the fees paid by local authorities and families, were capable of being a self-financing enterprise.

But the private equity firm was not prepared to be a long-term owner. Instead it saw an opportunity to make a quick profit by floating Southern Cross, as a public company, on the London stock market. In the process it collected £600 million of profits for itself and its wealthy investors. Unfortunately, the company it created was badly equipped to cope with the economic downturn that began with the 2007–2009 financial crisis. In the following years a combination of lack of investment, poor management and rising rents charged by landlords – some of which had also been sold off by Blackstone – brought Southern Cross to the brink, placing its 750 homes and 31,000 elderly and vulnerable residents at serious risk by mid-2011.

The Blackstone strategy had been to apply modern management techniques to a business that was unsuited to bear them. Although it could argue that Southern Cross had emerged intact from its period of private equity ownership, this actually proved very little: such a short period of ownership, in ideal economic conditions, was hardly an ideal test bed for a new management model that, as with every business, has to operate not just in good times but in adverse circumstances, too. It was highly questionable whether Blackstone and health care for the elderly in Britain was ever an ideal fit.

Blackstone's goal was to achieve a 'quick flip', at the end of which the homes could be sold back to the stock market at a big profit. Arguably, they were buying a robust business: care homes are in constant demand; they see a continuous flow of old people, largely funded by the state, and so offer a reliable source of income. The Blackstone model was, however, deeply flawed. It didn't allow for the fact that private sector landlords, some of whom operated from a company created by Blackstone, would raise rents in the face of the enveloping financial and economic catastrophe. It didn't allow for the fact that the squeeze on public finances would leave local authorities unable to meet any extra costs. In the event, Southern Cross soon found itself short of cash and the banks – reluctant to lend in the dire economic conditions of 2010–2011 – pulled the rug from under them.

In June 2011 the shares of the company were suspended on the London stock market and Southern Cross unilaterally cut the rents it paid to landlords by 30 per cent. As part of its effort to stave off bankruptcy it announced that it would be cutting 3,000 jobs out of its workforce of 44,000, a move that raised new questions about quality of care. In July 2011 249 of the 752 homes were rescued when landlord NHP announced it had reached a deal with Court Cavendish, a health care group run by Dr Chai Patel (former boss of the Priory chain of clinics). Another 250, or one-third of the homes, were taken back into ownership by the landlords who agreed to operate the homes. The fate of the final third, hit by low occupancy rates and high rents, remained unsettled.

The Southern Cross debacle demonstrates in its most extreme form the dangers of foreign ownership of a sensitive public service. There was, of course, nothing wrong in Blackstone pursuing profit – no company can survive without it. And clearly the criticism of its role stunned the private equity concern which – like all companies in its sector – prefers to conduct its affairs away from the glare of publicity. To offset negative media coverage it launched a public relations offensive in an effort to clarify its role. During a visit to the *Daily Mail* and in a statement posted on its website the firm said it could not be held responsible 'for the wider economic climate and controlled neither the debt levels nor any additional transactions entered into by the newly independent company (Southern Cross)'.

Nevertheless, it remains a fact that a big profit was made during a short period of ownership and that Southern Cross went into the financial crisis of 2007–2008 ill-equipped to weather challenging times. Blackstone did not step in to provide financial assistance to support the company or the damaged elderly residents.

At the care homes chain there was a balance to be struck between profit and public interest, something that is very difficult to sustain when the ultimate owners operate from headquarters in another country and are motivated by a desire for short-term gain. Unfortunately, that crucial connection between ownership and the end user of the services provided did not exist. Instead of serving UK citizens and consumers, the funds were there for the benefit of their owners, the investors and the managers, many of whom were highly incentivised to make the best possible returns.

Infrastructure specialist David Lee of City law firm Allen & Overy – part of the 'magic circle' with a lock on many of Britain's biggest corporate deals – questioned the status of the transactions: 'There is an unarticulated worry about who invests in infrastructure funds, and also concern about whether ownership of an asset has an impact on its operation.'

The Southern Cross experience is not unique, though it has probably garnered the most press and Parliamentary attention. Similar problems have cropped up in the deregulated utilities market. Utilities have a direct relationship with almost every household in the nation. Again, the same basic tension exists: the need of the operating company to make a profit while simultaneously honouring its obligation to provide customers with reliable power supplies, high water quality and sewage and waste disposal.

The existence of such regulators as Ofgem for the power industry and Ofwat for the water industry represents official recognition that in a free-for-all market the customer these days needs extra protection. Their general ineffectiveness, though, suggests that the balance of responsibility and power is not all that it should be.

In the early days of deregulation that followed the privatisation of so many of the nation's vital services in the 1990s, a large percentage of the owners of the regional electricity distribution companies were American. US utility companies, who were very tightly regulated at home, were attracted to the free and easy environment of the UK and saw an opportunity to make some easy profits and ship them back to the US. In the process they brought with them American-style remuneration packages for directors which saw many former government employees turned into boardroom 'fat cats' overnight – much to the distress of ordinary consumers.

The decade 1987 to 1997 saw the profits of the electricity industry soar from £249 million to £1.5 billion according to data collected by the Institute of Fiscal Studies. A similar pattern was seen in the privatised water sector where in the years 1990 to 1997–1998 profits climbed by 147 per cent. Over the same period the pay of the highest paid water company executives soared by between 50 per cent and 200 per cent with the highest paid director at Anglian Water seeing his pay climb from £126,000 to £378,000. A similar pattern was seen across the industry. Post-privatisation, directors' pay across the utilities was estimated to rise by 12 per cent a year against 3.1 per cent for employees. The focus of public anger turned out to be the unfortunate chief executive of British Gas, Cedric Brown, who in 1994, having secured a 75 per cent pay rise to £475,000, was the subject of public opprobrium. Leaders from the GMB union paraded a live pig outside the company's packed annual general meeting in Docklands – it was intended as a symbol of Brown's perceived greed.

The blue touch paper had been lit and the new Chancellor of the Exchequer Gordon Brown, looking for an easy hit in his 1997 budget, saw the utility companies as a target. In a desperate move to raise money to fulfil Labour's manifesto commitments without raising income tax, he decided – with the assistance of (since defunct) accountants Arthur Andersen – to make a dawn raid on utility companies. In doing so, he was confident that his actions would receive wide support from a public uneasy about foreign ownership, big profits and dividends for investors and critical of the high salaries the bosses of power utilities were receiving.

In his first Budget, therefore, Brown imposed a 'windfall tax', raising more than £6 billion in the process. The tax hit came as a shock to the utilities and frightened off the foreign owners. Their reaction was to discard their 'long-term' investments in British power generation almost as quickly as they had been made and to head back to the other side of the Atlantic.

But their departure did not herald a new era of British ownership. Instead, a new wave of buyers came to the fore, and by the time the buying frenzy was over, five out of Britain's big seven energy suppliers had fallen under the control of a different set of foreign owners. By a strange ironic quirk, several of the second generation of owners from abroad were state controlled. Nationalised utilities which had been privatised only a few years before were now effectively in state hands again – though the state in question was no longer Britain. As prime minister, Tony Blair was unconcerned. His stated view in March 2006 was: 'Liberalised energy markets and more open markets are good for business and for consumers' rights across Europe.'

The fate of London Electricity was typical. Bought by US firm Entergy in 1996 for £1.3 billion, it was sold two years later to French state-owned EDF (Electricité de France) for £1.9 billion.

EDF later moved to buy up two small nearby power distributors and merged them into a new company, EDF Energy. In 2009 it went on to win control of Britain's nuclear power generators.

National Power, one of the UK's biggest generators with 6 million customers, was split in two in the year 2000. The domestic British operation was renamed Innogy and the global business called International Power. Both companies had separate London Stock Exchange share quotations. Innogy moved swiftly to buy the regional electricity distribution firm Yorkshire Power from US owners American Power and Xcel Energy in 2001 for £1.8 billion. Less than a year later Innogy and its new Yorkshire offshoot were swallowed by Germany's RWE for £5.3 billion and renamed RWE npower. The now German-owned firm would trade in the UK under the name npower.

The UK's second major generator Powergen was purchased for £5.1 billion by the German power colossus E.ON in 2002. It would go on to take a 30 per cent stake in London Array, the large and highly subsidised wind farm project in the Thames Estuary. In a few short years Germany's RWE and E.ON had gained a substantial hold over the British energy market. As part of an effort to make them seem less foreign, the two German outfits took up sponsorship of quintessentially British sporting events including cricket Test matches and the FA Cup.

Finally, in August 2010, International Power, the global arm of what had once been National Power, also ended up in foreign hands. International Power had been successful in selling modern generation plants to developing countries and had become an excellent source of foreign earnings, even though it was up against much bigger competitors. But French giant GDF Suez – itself 35 per cent government controlled – swallowed it up. Once again, a privatised UK firm was being semi-nationalised by a foreign owner.

One consequence of all this deal-making was the abandonment of an important principle that had been established some years before. At the time of electricity privatisation the government had deliberately separated the distributors, such as London Electricity and Yorkshire Power, from the generators, such as Powergen, with the aim of ensuring that there was a true measure of competition between the different distributors. But over a relatively short period, overseas companies, including EDF, RWE and E.ON, were allowed to put Humpty Dumpty back together again. Indeed there was a real concentration of power muscle. E.ON, through its subsidiary Powergen, for example, ended up providing power and gas to 9 million British customers, making it the country's second largest electricity and gas provider after Centrica – the UK energy group that owns British Gas.

France and Germany were not the only European countries to get in on the act. In 2006 Spain's Iberdrola swooped to buy Scottish Power, which had been badly weakened by a foolish foray into the US where it came unstuck as a result of tough Californian utility regulation. The message from Iberdrola's investment banking backers was that it was a great fit, though the exact connection between Southern Spain and Scotland was never made exactly clear.

By 2010 just 34 per cent of the fuel for the UK economy remained in British hands; 32 per cent was under French control; 27 per cent in the hands of German enterprises; and 7 per cent under Spain's command.

Not everyone has remained sanguine about this turn of events. In early 2011, on a train journey from London to Cardiff, I bumped into Ed Wallis, formerly of Powergen and one of the grand old men of the British energy industry. An ebullient figure with swept back hair, he had at first relished the economic

freedom afforded by being cut loose from government, but when
I spoke to him he seemed strangely diminished by what had
subsequently happened to his industry. He was clearly concerned
that in a world of free and open capital markets – when any
company can bid for another – the authorities had been too
supine when it came to foreign takeovers of key British utilities
and insufficiently questioning of whether there might be any
unforeseen consequences.

Alistair Buchanan, a former City analyst who became head of
energy regulator Ofgem, is similarly concerned. A slim, restless
figure who is seeking to plan future strategy and direction for the
industry, he constantly questions the behaviour of those he
regulates, their treatment of the consumer (especially the least well
off), the way the industry sets prices and its long-term thinking on
future energy investment.

He seeks to use his office as a 'bully pulpit', going public whenever he can with complaints and deploying his powers as
judiciously as possible. But it is a constant battle against remote,
absent landlords shielded from public opprobrium in their
Continental fortresses.

One of his principal concerns is that foreign-owned utilities
have a record of instantly passing on price increases to UK
consumers when oil and gas prices are rising, but failing to adjust
them downwards fast enough – if at all – when wholesale prices are
falling. A 2011 'Retail Market Review' by the regulator Ofgem
found, for instance, that UK-owned British Gas (part of Centrica)
'set an average electricity price below the other Big Six' across most
regions of the country. Scottish & Southern, which is one of two
power companies to remain in British hands, decided in October
2011 to sell all its power into the open market. It hoped that by
being more responsive to changes in the wholesale markets it could

reintroduce an element of competition and contribute to bringing prices down at times of fuel plenty.

There are other problems, too, with foreign ownership in this sector. Utility companies with an international reach can very easily transfer profits from one part of the world to another rather than reinvest them in infrastructure, service and lower prices in the host country. In 2011 it was disclosed that Iberdrola, the Spanish owners of Scottish Power, used a cash surplus at its Scottish Power subsidiary to make a ten-year loan of £800 million to its sister company in the United States – a pioneer of wind technology.

To avoid allegations of cross-subsidy the 2009 loan was made at commercial interest rates. Disclosure of the transfer came just weeks after Scottish Power had raised the prices of energy supplied to its customers. It sparked immediate controversy in Scotland, which has seen an average rise of 40 per cent in energy bills since 2007. In contrast Iberdrola's American consumers have had their gas and electricity bills frozen since the mid-1990s until the imposition of a 4 to 8 per cent rise in 2011.

Glasgow MP John Robertson was among those expressing his outrage:

I was shocked and very angry to learn this and it seems beyond the pale to be hiking prices in the UK when the company has lent £800 million. It is in no one's interest to have energy companies milking the British consumer at a time when households are struggling to make ends meet.

Foreign ownership of the UK's power supplies also raises issues of politics and energy security. What happens when an international power company suddenly experiences a squeeze on supply? In the winter of 2005, for example, gas came under pressure when Russia cut off natural gas supply lines through the Ukraine. The European Union, including the UK, was at the time obtaining 20 per cent of its gas from Russia, with 80 per cent passing through pipelines in Ukraine.

Britain's fuel needs were partly satisfied by gas passing through the Ruhrgas pipeline largely controlled by E.ON, one of Britain's major energy suppliers. It was not the best position to be in. Reflecting on events the newsletter Energy Bulletin noted in 2009: 'The UK government was facing the very real prospects of gas cuts as domestic production was shrinking and inadequate plans for import and gas storage were in place.' The 2005–2006 disruption demonstrated how vulnerable Britain's energy supplies are to global political rows and the way in which foreign ownership of energy suppliers can be to the UK's disadvantage.

This is particularly true in the UK now that Russia has become involved in the supply of our energy needs through supplies piped across the Ukraine and Europe to UK consumers. In 2006 the state-owned Russian gas conglomerate Gazprom expressed an interest in buying British Gas's parent company Centrica, gaining access to its 15.7 million UK customers. The move came in the wake of the Kremlin's efforts to use its energy resources as a political weapon in its battle with troublesome neighbours in Ukraine and Georgia. Alexander Medvedev, deputy chairman of Gazprom, publicly revealed that Centrica was a takeover target. The approach rightly sparked fears of energy supplies being used as a political weapon, as Moscow had done when turning off the gas taps to the Ukraine in a dispute the year before.

Tony Blair, who had presided over the sale overseas of so much of Britain's energy industry, was unfazed by the Gazprom approach. He ruled out the possibility that the government might block the bid, telling political allies that Britain had to face down the wave of 'economic patriotism' blocking cross-border deals elsewhere in Europe. The argument against narrow economic patriotism and protectionism was laudable enough. But, arguably, Blair was allowing Britain to become a test bed for a radical new ownership pattern which directly impacted on the nature of Britain's energy security. Shares in Centrica climbed in response to the possibility.

However, despite the Medvedev threat and Blair's backing for open markets, no such offer ever materialised. Had it done so, Centrica chairman Sir Roger Carr is of the view that there were other people in and around government, including Lord (Peter) Mandelson, Alistair Darling and Blair's successor Gordon Brown, who would have wanted the transaction to be closely examined, and it was likely that it would have been blocked. In the event Carr – veteran of the takeover wars – never received any personal approach from Medvedev or his associates.

Alistair Darling has expressed strong reservations about direct Russian involvement in Britain's gas supply:

> Suppose it was Gazprom you were getting your gas from. And as we know Gazprom goes on and off just because the pipe's cracked. I think there is a huge issue and it's security. Frankly, as we know, a very recent memory, if you lose power it is catastrophic. Remember the blackout in London a few years ago? It was an accident but it paralysed half the City and it's terrifying.

Nevertheless, that doesn't mean that an arrangement between Britain and Russia could never be countenanced. One could imagine, for example, that were power supplies to become stretched, a British government might well consider allowing Centrica to be bought in exchange for a guarantee of future natural gas supplies secured through a minority share stake and board role at Gazprom. Immediate crises have a way of leading to unlikely alliances.

Leaving Russia aside for one moment, concerns could also be raised about other suppliers of gas to the UK. Qatar and Algeria, for example, operate in less than peaceful areas of the world. Were another energy crisis to occur on the scale of that of the 1970s, Britain would be in real trouble. The big Continental energy firms such as RWE and E.ON doubtless feel more of an obligation to keep the Ruhr supplied rather than, say, Tyneside, if push came to shove. And if that seems like scaremongering, it's worth bearing in mind that in the Arctic winter of 2010–2011, the gas supplies through the Langeled UK–Norway pipeline were substantially reduced because the Norwegians – inevitably and understandably – prioritised themselves and their closest trading partners.

To an extent Britain is cushioned at present by North Sea oil and gas production, which fulfils 38 per cent of the nation's annual requirements. But the supplies are dwindling year by year and much of the Brent crude is sold on the global market rather than consumed at home, making the UK rather less self-sufficient than it might appear at first blush.

Nuclear power is potentially an even more contentious issue. For some years it seemed a side concern. Many Labour MPs, and indeed the country as a whole, had become deeply suspicious of nuclear power. They were sceptical about its safety record, particularly in the aftermath of the accidents at Three Mile Island in America and Chernobyl in the former Soviet Union (a scepticism that returned in March 2011 when the nuclear facility at

Fukushima in Japan was badly damaged by an earthquake and tsunami). They also pointed to the high costs of disposing of nuclear waste, the long-term environmental problems this might entail, and the huge price tags attached to decommissioning an ageing fleet of existing nuclear plants. One way or another, it looked as though its importance in the provision of the UK's electricity would decline over time.

In the lead up to the 2005 election the Labour government were anxious to keep nuclear power off the agenda. At a private dinner for City writers hosted by the Energy Minister Michael O'Brien at a central London hotel, also attended by leading civil servants and industrialists, it was made patently clear that future nuclear energy investment was not being discussed. There was no private sector money available, and the government was not prepared to provide a new nuclear subsidy. In future, the focus would be on alternatives such as wind and wave power.

In this environment, it seemed entirely logical that the government would want to step away from any involvement in nuclear energy. So it came as no surprise when, in February 2006, the state-owned British Nuclear Fuels Limited (BNFL), announced that it had sold its power station construction arm, Westinghouse, to Japan's Toshiba corporation. There was little public opposition. The Prospect union, which represents several thousand engineers, scientists and managers at 22 sites, attacked the sale as 'robbing Britain of new-build expertise', but their worries were ignored. The $5.4 billion received was a welcome bonus for the Exchequer.

While all this was going on, however, a counter-movement to the anti-nuclear lobby was building. Paradoxically, given past history, it was motivated by environmental concerns. Previously many had viewed nuclear power as the enemy of the planet. Now there were those who argued that it was a considerably cleaner form of energy than carbon-based alternatives. Moreover, there were also those who pointed out that unless Britain took dramatic action, and reinvested in the nuclear option, it would soon face a major power crisis as existing nuclear power plants were moth-balled and other sources – for example, oil – became evermore expensive.

These considerations make Labour's decision to allow the sale of Westinghouse more questionable. Westinghouse, originally an American firm, was just one of a handful of designers, manufacturers and builders of new nuclear plants around the world and it was being disposed of just as nations across the world – from Finland to China – were looking for cleaner energy and so investing in new nuclear. Ownership of Westinghouse had offered Britain the opportunity to become a leader in a booming sector. Instead, it opted to take a back seat.

Consequently, when Gordon Brown succeeded Tony Blair as prime minister in June 2007 he found himself having to look abroad when deciding what to do about the government's stake in British Energy, owner of the country's legacy nuclear reactors and the best sites for future new nuclear development. An announce-ment to sell BE was made in 2008, and a year later a £12.5 billion deal was done with the French state-owned EDF. The French company, also one of Britain's biggest power suppliers, announced that it was planning to build four new nuclear power stations in the UK.

By this time, though, some official disquiet had clearly set in. Shortly before the deal was done I can remember being in Downing Street for a briefing from Chancellor Alistair Darling on the latest developments in the global financial crisis. On the way out I spotted Roger Carr, chairman of Centrica, and his chief executive Sam Laidlaw emerging from Number 10. Within days it was disclosed to shareholders that Centrica would be taking a 10 per cent stake in British Energy. Centrica's involvement, encouraged by the government, meant that there would now be a large, publicly quoted British shareholder to provide a counterbalance to French ownership. Even so, since EDF was now the company with nuclear expertise it was inevitable that French companies such as AREVA would get the lion's share of development contracts, and that British companies, such as Rolls-Royce, would become subcontractors to French masters.

Some would argue that the constant buying and selling of utility companies in Britain is part of the natural capitalist order of things. But, as I have suggested, it is a risky strategy, which takes absolutely no account of what might happen in the future. It is classic short-termism. Significantly, too, it's not a strategy that has been adopted by other countries. In Germany, for example, the big power generators E.ON and RWE are regarded as national champions and enjoy the privileges of this status. E.ON was created out of a merger of two of the country's biggest energy groups VEBA and VIAG and is now the largest publicly owned energy supplier in the world. As the owner of Ruhrgas it has huge clout across the Continent, providing pipeline services in more than 20 countries.

RWE, which can trace its history back to 1898, is the second largest electricity generator in Europe, with a reach across the Continent to the Czech Republic and the Netherlands. It has become so powerful an influence over Europe's energy supplies that it has been involved in a long tussle with the European Commission as to whether it should unbundle its generation from some of its distribution and transmission in the interests of competition. Its shares, like those of E.ON, are quoted on the Frankfurt stock exchange. Both companies operate through supply agreements with Germany's corporate sector and municipalities.

The sheer scale and spread of their operations makes them part of Germany's industrial architecture and all but immune to takeover. Moreover, they are afforded legislative protections, which are elaborate and complicated, which has made it all but impossible for UK firms like Centrica to compete with them on their Continental territory. Both RWE and E.ON have also established a special relationship with the Russian gas supplier Gazprom and have a number of joint supply and pipeline ventures which has helped to ensure preferential treatment and security of supplies. The intense focus on Continental markets also means that the European owners (RWE, E.ON, EDF and Iberdrola) tend to be far more reluctant to rebuild the UK infrastructure.

The US has in recent times dabbled with deregulation (the rules concerning which vary from state to state and municipality to municipality), but with strings attached. British players have not found the going easy. In 2000, for example, Britain's Scottish Power, having bought PacifiCorp (which covered California, Oregon and Washington), found itself struggling to meet the demands of US rules and regulations. After incurring heavy losses it managed to dispose of the prize to Warren Buffett's MidAmerican Energy Holdings in 2005 in a deal valued at $5.1 billion.

Another UK firm, National Grid, invested in New York state and the Eastern Seaboard. But it soon discovered that pricing and investment decisions are strictly policed by state and city authorities and that prices cannot be raised by company fiat. Instead any proposed price increase is subjected to public hearings in which all interested groups have their say. The states demand full disclosure of internal financial information including details of the costs and lifestyles of executives. Investigations by the New

York Public Service Commission of National Grid's operations in the state found potential over-charging of expenses of $26 million. The result of this and requests for price increases in other states, including New Hampshire, was that National Grid has been knocked back in its efforts to force through price increases. Only Centrica, which has focused on selling power into unregulated markets like Texas, challenging incumbents on price and service and buying into its own sources of supply, has managed to operate in North America without getting fingers burned.

The net effect has been that while America in theory welcomes foreign buyers, in practice many of the states and localities place such firm controls on intruders that these effectively act as a deterent to overseas involvement. Arguably, in Britain we have the worst of all worlds: overseas ownership and no real accountability or constraint on price rises. Increases in tariffs are frequent and sometimes look arbitrary and have been a big factor in pushing up overall levels of inflation.

True, UK energy is still cheaper than on the Continent, where it can cost up to 20 to 30 per cent more. But this has much to do with the North Sea oil cushion. It is not a permanent given. Nor do current prices take account of required future investment in infrastructure. Among the biggest investments that will soon be required is the £200 billion which British-owned National Grid says is needed to update the nation's distribution network to accommodate power generated from conventional sources, from renewables (such as wind farms), and from a new generation of giant French-built nuclear power stations. The burden of paying for this will fall on UK consumers, through surcharges on their quarterly bills. Much of the benefit, by contrast, will accrue to overseas-owned generators and power firms.

The influence that Europe's giant power companies have over

our daily lives was demonstrated in January 2012 when French government-controlled EDF Energy became the first of the big six companies operating in Britain to recognise a fall in the cost of wholesale gas (largely as a result of a mild winter in 2011–2012) and cut its prices by 5 per cent from February. In effect the company was reversing one-third of the 15.4 per cent price increase it had imposed on domestic and business consumers as recently as November 2011. As Adam Scorer, director of policy and external affairs at the watchdog Consumer Focus noted: 'The cut is not enormous given the scale of the increases last year but it creates some important momentum.'

EDF's action may have appeared to be an act of leadership, as other suppliers including market leader British Gas (owned by UK-based Centrica) would follow suit in 24 hours. The timing was, however, useful in both political and public relations terms. EDF recognised that the heat would be on from the regulator for price cuts after a 22 per cent decline in wholesale prices since September. It was also aware that the new annual survey by consumer watchdog Which? had found that of the big six energy groups, one, British-owned SSE (formerly Scottish and Southern Energy), received a satisfaction score greater than 51 per cent.

EDF also had other good reasons for keeping Britain's coalition government on side. As the dominant shareholder in Britain's nuclear energy provider British Energy, EDF is involved in detailed discussions with the UK authorities over the future guaranteed price for power generated by new-build nuclear power stations. In effect it is asking the authorities for a nuclear subsidy, which will eventually be passed on to consumers through an extra charge on their monthly or quarterly energy bills. If the new build goes ahead, as was widely expected at the start of 2012, the government will be committing itself to a subsidy to a French state-controlled company paid for by UK taxpayers' money. In such a context a small reduction in gas prices, a fraction of the reduction of the cost in wholesale markets, must be regarded as no more than a gesture. What it doesn't suggest is that EDF is particularly sensitive to the UK consumer per se.

International ownership has been equally problematical for Britain's water companies, where the supposedly tidy free market structures, put in place at the time of privatisation, have not stood the test of time that well.

Back in the 1990s, there seemed to be a compelling case for privatising Britain's water companies. They had a guaranteed customer base that would appeal to investors. And they also needed major new investment. Many of the country's cities were served by pipes and sewage systems that dated back to Victorian times and that urgently needed repairing or replacing. The government of the day was keen to remove the financial obligations involved from public expenditure commitments.

One of the jewels in the crown was Thames Water. The reach and assets of the water company may have been dilapidated but they were vast. Thames Water had 8.5 million water customers and 13.5 million waste water clients, and operated 100 water treatment plants, 290 pumping stations and 235 reservoirs. So it was no surprise when in 2001, a decade after privatisation, it was snapped up by Germany's RWE, one of Europe's largest power utilities. At the time RWE was seeking to build a water empire, on both sides of the Atlantic, to match its strength in the power sector.

The company proved a highly valuable asset to the German giant and by 2005 Thames Water profits were soaring. Profits climbed 30 per cent to £346 million in 2005 with the help of a 21 per cent price rise imposed on its customers with the approval of the notoriously useless regulator Ofwat. The jump in earnings was achieved despite a failure to develop or fix the ancient infrastructure. In fact, from the time of the RWE takeover, Thames Water failed all regulatory leakage targets. By 2005, its pipe infrastructure in Britain was in such disrepair that it leaked a disgraceful 196 million gallons a day.

Things came to a head during the long summer and serious drought of 2006. As lawns turned yellow and plants in parks and gardens drooped, water rationing was introduced: Thames customers were banned from watering their lawns and washing their cars. While Thames Water's German owners could scarcely be blamed for an act of God, the fact that they had done so little to stop the haemorrhaging of water from the system became a public scandal. And things weren't made any better for them when the *Daily Mail* decided to run a series of articles on what it regarded as the uncaring attitude of Thames Water's absentee owners.

The first piece to be run revealed that the five men controlling 'Britain's most wasteful water company from Essen in Germany were being paid a staggering £20 million a year. Chief executive Harry Roels earned £6.3 million; vice-president Jan Zilius, £3.9 million; Labour director Alwin Fitting, £900,000; vice-president Berthold Bonekamp, £3.3 million; and finance chief Klaus Sturany, £5.9 million.'

The *Daily Mail*'s Natalie Clark pursued RWE's directors to their home districts in Holland and Germany. In Laren in Holland, where Roels lived, she found that water supplies were plentiful and the sprinklers were on full power at weekends, spraying the immaculately tended, lush green front lawns. At the back of the properties, swimming pools were comfortably full. It also transpired that while the average Thames Water customer was paying £265 a year, in tranquil Laren residents paid well under half that amount for a first-class modern supply network – a model of Dutch efficiency.

'The scandalous profits from Thames Water help him maintain his luxurious lifestyle in Laren alongside the other Dutch tycoons, film stars and TV presenters who are his neighbours. Everyone in Utrecht aspires to live in Laren, but only those with millions are able to,' wrote Clark.

The ghastly publicity forced Philip Fletcher, director-general of Ofwat, up until then a largely ineffectual industry regulator, to confront the issue head-on. Describing the situation as 'totally unacceptable' and pointing out that the water leaked from Thames Water's pipes could supply 2.8 million homes each day, Ofwat accused the company of profiteering. It added that the failure of Thames to curb the leakages had contributed to water shortages in the south and threatened to increase the need for hosepipe bans and other restrictions in future years.

RWE was taken aback by the criticism. It wasn't used to investigative reporters poking around in its backyard, nor had it felt the heat of the regulator's wrath before. 'We are unhappy and disappointed with the situation,' it announced contritely. 'We are investing £500,000 a day to reduce leakage and are convinced our colleagues at Thames Water are doing their best to modernise the system.'

In public, RWE was taking its medicine. Behind the scenes, and despite all its words of commitment, it now plotted its exit from a market that had proven to be such a public relations disaster. It did not, however, leave empty-handed. Over its five years of ownership RWE had paid out £1 billion in dividends to its mainly German shareholders, including a final payment of £216 million.

The initial plan was to float the company, valued at between £7 billion and £8 billion, on the London Stock Exchange within 18 months. But the adverse publicity took its toll and RWE decided to speed up the process with a trade auction. The new owner, also from overseas, came in the shape of Kemble Water, a company controlled by Australian infrastructure fund Macquarie. Its £8 billion bid, at a 20 per cent premium on the group's value, won the day, beating off an offer from Qatar's Investment Authority.

Nothing at Macquarie, a private equity fund with a reputation for being too clever by half, was ever straightforward. As the BBC's Robert Peston pointed out:

> When Macquarie buys assets, it tends to load them up with borrowings. Thames Water has a very big investment programme to implement and regulators will look to check that the debt on that programme to improve pipelines will be paid.

A lightning strike series of deals saw it first dispose of South East Water to Australia's Hastings Funds Management. South East then merged with Mid Kent Water in 2007, under the ownership of a newly formed Hastings Diversified Utilities Fund and United Utilities of Australia. Elsewhere, Wessex Water passed into the hands of Malaysia-based YTL Power International in 2002, and France's Veolia owned three water companies in south-east England.

Britain's water supply remains dominated by foreign owners from Europe and the Pacific region. In August 2011 one of the remaining independent companies, Northumbrian Water, was bought by the Hong Kong tycoon Li Ka-shing through Cheung Kong Infrastructure Holdings for £2.4 billion, raising hopes of a further round of overseas incursions. The Thames Water experience, however, does show that even foreign owners – like RWE – are not totally impervious to consumer power and poor media coverage. It also galvanised a sleepy regulator into action and proved that Ofwat, like Ofgem in the power sector, can be a significant counter-balance to a company's desire for profit.

Far from speeding up investment, however, the initial experience of foreign ownership of the water companies suggests they had more interest in extracting profits and shareholder value than in improving the reliability and quality of UK water supplies and sewerage disposal.

Whether the issue is water or energy, we should never doubt the capacity of overseas or foreign investors to uproot in challenging times or to make life for British consumers and businesses more difficult. In Arctic weather, such as in the winter of 2010–2011, even 'friendly' foreign-owned companies have tended to place British consumers low on their list of priorities. When it comes to other world powers, Russia has already demonstrated its willing-ness to use energy as a political tool. Other gas suppliers, including Qatar and Algeria, operate in less than peaceful neighbourhoods. In early 2012 Iran's threat to close the Strait of Hormuz in the Arabian Gulf, through which more than 20 per cent of the world's traded oil supplies pass, sent market prices for oil soaring.

Similarly, the revolutions across North Africa and the Middle East – which have seen governments swept from power in energy-rich nations like Libya – underline the fragility of oil and gas supplies. In an age of energy shortages, upheavals in the Middle East and North Africa and persistent tensions with Russia and China, retaining a measure of control and influence over strategic industries remains important. The UK has been able in the past to rely on North Sea supplies, and on the knowledge that the country still sits on a vast amount of untapped coal (even if we have dismantled the extraction industry). The ease with which foreign powers could disrupt the nation's energy supplies, bringing the economy to a shuddering halt, is frightening.

When I spoke with former Thatcher government adviser and chairman of P&O Lord Sterling at his West End office in 2011, he left no doubt about his deep-seated concerns about energy security:

There are only eight days of natural gas held in this country. Some 50 per cent of it comes via France, the rest from Norway, etc. If that gets disrupted one day what the bloody hell would we do? I was in the middle of the oil [delivery] tanker strike a decade or so ago when P&O did the deliveries on behalf of Shell. The country ground to a stop in no time. Take LNG (Liquid Natural Gas). If the Iranians mined the Gulf and took out the Suez Canal, which could easily be done, the effect not just on our supplies, the stock market, oil prices and so forth would be dramatic. In 24 hours to 48 hours we would be all over the place. That is even before we consider cyber warfare, which could also be hugely critical.

Along every link of the supply chain, down to the power companies that deliver electricity and gas to our homes, Britain has neglected the importance of energy security. It has allowed four of our big six energy companies to fall under Continental ownership, where the UK is regarded as a useful profit centre rather than of critical importance. It has toyed with alternative forms of energy, such as wind power, pretending that these could close the gap, but in the process has merely kidded itself. When Gordon Brown's government suddenly changed tack and decided to address the crisis by encouraging nuclear power, it did so by selling off our fleet of plants to EDF with British-owned Centrica a minority shareholder.

The coalition government of 2010 was initially less than enthusiastic about nuclear power. The Lib Dem energy secretary Chris Huhne, for example, argued that the nuclear option could only be justified if it did not require state subsidy. When it became apparent, however, that investment in new nuclear would not be possible unless the taxpayer picked up some of the bill, through guaranteed tariffs for the power produced, there was a change of heart. A White Paper was duly published in July 2011, revealing plans to invest £110 billion in nuclear energy and, in the process, replacing a quarter of the nation's nuclear power stations by 2030.

Even then, the UK's nuclear future is far from assured. Problems with some of French-owned EDF's other nuclear facilities in France and in Finland means that UK nuclear has moved down the list of priorities. And if it does all go ahead, the expertise for a new generation of nuclear reactors will come from EDF and the French engineering and contracting group AREVA. Ceding control of our nuclear destiny to foreign owners has added yet another layer of uncertainty to the nation's energy future.

7

The Export of Transport

In December 2010 Britain was in the grip of heavy snow. Many roads were impassable and airports had ground to a halt. Heathrow, in particular, as I noted in the *Daily Mail* at the time, had been turned into something akin to a Third World refugee camp with thousands of passengers trapped for days in an airport all but paralysed by snow. It was a public relations disaster for the foreign-run British Airports Authority, coming as it did only a few months after the fallout from an Icelandic volcano had grounded much of northern Europe's aeroplanes.

In the wake of the Heathrow chaos, the social and political commentator Melanie Phillips wrote in *The Spectator*:

> The British public is now at the mercy of indifferent foreign companies to keep the national show on the road. It's all part of Labour's truly abominable legacy of wrecking the UK in the cause of realising some brave new, utterly changed world.

BAA has had something of a chequered recent history. One of Britain's corporate crown jewels, at its height it owned and operated airports that handled 63 per cent of travellers going into and out of the UK. In Scotland, BAA handled 86 per cent of all air travellers, managing airports at Glasgow, Edinburgh and Aberdeen. In London, the commercial hub of the nation, the number of air travellers through BAA airports stood at 92 per cent.

BAA was privatised by the Thatcher government amid enormous demand for the new company's shares, placing a value of £1.225 billion on the firm. Under the leadership of its first chief executive Colin Matthews and then his successor Sir John Egan it expanded rapidly, adding Southampton Airport to its portfolio and winning contracts to run airports from Harrisburg USA to Melbourne in Australia. In 1998 Heathrow was boosted by the opening of the £450 million Heathrow Express. In 2002 the chair was taken over by the upright investment banker Marcus Agius, who stepped up from deputy chairman. It turned out to be a fateful move for Agius, who amid the overseas takeover fever of the noughties found himself at the heart of one of the most contentious of all deals done in the heady years of the mid-2000s.

In June 2006 a consortium headed by the Spanish construction company Ferrovial made a successful £10.6 billion bid. At the time, the *Independent* described the deal as 'the most dramatic example yet of the way in which strategic UK assets are falling to overseas bidders'. The *Economist* magazine took a fairly bullish view: 'The Spanish firm Ferrovial,' it argued, 'can hardly do a worse job of running London's Heathrow Airport than did BAA.'

In theory, the deal should have opened the way for much-needed investment. Heathrow needed to be brought up to date, and there was a generally accepted perception that it also needed to be expanded. Unfortunately, the acquisition left a debt mountain that was still proving virtually unclimbable five years later. It also left key airports in the control of a company with little experience of the sector. Ferrovial is essentially a family-controlled Spanish construction group with no experience at all of running a consumer-facing enterprise on the scale of one of Europe's biggest hub airports.

Whereas in the case of Thames Water the regulator eventually proved quite effective as a counter-balance, the airport regulator, the Civil Aviation Authority, proved rather less effectual with BAA. Its expertise lay largely in upholding safety standards, and in fact for a number of decades it had quite a cosy relationship with BAA, and to a lesser extent Heathrow's main user British Airways. Asking difficult questions was consequently not part of its DNA. Nor did it have the broad economic mandate of the other regulators of privatised enterprises. When the prospect of a buyout by Ferrovial came up, the CAA did – as a result of media pressure – take a look at the amount of debt Ferrovial was raising for the buyout, but decided it lacked the tools and authority to intervene. This did not augur well for the future. A highly indebted corporation that was clearly hoping to run the business for cash, and hopeful of some big building contracts in the process, found itself in charge of a complex organisation that desperately needed investment.

Over the next few years, London's other airports – Gatwick in Sussex and Stansted in Essex – groaned under the weight of passenger numbers. Overcrowding at the terminal became part of the experience of flying, and the often appalling facilities – from the state of the toilets to adequate space for security checks – became legendary. As for Heathrow itself, when BAA did eventually deliver a shining new Heathrow Terminal 5 to British Airways, poor planning and major teething problems turned the launch of a prestige project into a national farce.

In the ten years spent getting the project through its approval phases and turning it into reality, Frankfurt increased its number of runways from two to four, while Amsterdam's Schiphol developed itself as an effective alternative hub to Heathrow. It is also worth noting that while British airports have a tendency to grind to a halt whenever there are adverse weather conditions, airports such as Frankfurt and Zurich – both of which experience extreme weather – are rarely closed as a result.

The CAA may have been the dog that failed to bark, but the Competition Commission, besieged by complaints about BAA's ruthless monopoly-style practices, was less easily satisfied. In April 2007, it launched an inquiry into BAA's dominant market position, questioning whether its control of seven key airports amounted to an unfair monopoly. BAA had been able to operate in much the same way for 40 years without official intervention, as a result of weak regulation by the CAA and the cosy relationship between the airport operator and British Airways. The Competition Commission decided in 2009 that the new owners Ferrovial would have to give up some of its stranglehold on British aviation.

In the event, the company was forced to divest 10 per cent of its 56 per cent holding in BAA and to sell off Gatwick (which it did in 2009) and Stansted, as well as either Glasgow or Edinburgh. The latter was put up for sale in the autumn of 2011 with the owners aiming to collect £600 million for the asset. Gatwick was bought by American investment group Global Infrastructure Partners (an investment consortium that included the South Korean National Pensions Fund) for £1.51 billion. Like Heathrow, Gatwick struggled with snow in December 2010 and had to close operations for 48 hours. It turned out that the airport had under-invested in snow-clearing equipment – it then went on to import second-hand equipment from Switzerland.

Few commentators have much sympathy for Ferrovial. In taking over BAA it overextended itself, and ended up running a company in a way that served neither the British economy nor the British traveller well. Even those in favour of foreign ownership are dubious about Ferrovial's record. 'By and large foreign ownership is a good thing,' Tim Ambler of the London Business School told me. 'A takeover only happens when an incoming group of businessmen believe they can run an organisation better than the existing group.' However, he went on to say, 'Ferrovial running the British Airports Authority is a rare example of when a foreign group come in and get it wrong.'

If foreign ownership of Britain's airports has been something of a disaster, the record of foreign involvement in Britain's railways is more equivocal – not least because the rail service can hardly be said to have thrived when it was under exclusively British control. The old British Rail was notoriously inefficient, its customer service legendary for its grudging nature and its safety record mixed. Moreover, there was little government money around for investment in station modernisation, electrification, modern signalling systems and up-to-date rolling stock.

Margaret Thatcher's privatisation programme of the 1980s was followed by significant reforms under her successor John Major in the early 1990s. Major's government decided that the best way to improve the railways was to introduce an element of competition into prices. It opted for a threefold approach: Railtrack (subsequently Network Rail) would control the lines; franchisees would run the trains on a regional basis; newly created Rolling Stock Operating Companies (known as the ROSCOs) would lease the trains and carriages to the franchisees. In this way, it was hoped, the lines would be modernised, rolling stock and stations improved, and customers presented with better service and more choice.

Problems with this approach surfaced in the late 1990s when fatal accidents at Southall in 1997 and Ladbroke Grove in 1999 showed up Railtrack's shortcomings when it came to overseeing the infrastructure of a fragmented rail network. The Hatfield crash on 17 October 2000, in which four people died, turned out to be the defining moment for Railtrack, exposing the company's shortcomings in maintenance and engineering, which had been sold off to private contractors. All this, together with the spiralling costs of the West Coast Main Line modernisation programme, pushed Railtrack into loss although it still paid a dividend.

Transport Secretary Stephen Byers thought it would be a big, easy political win if he took the company back into public ownership, and a year after Hatfield he applied to the High Court to put the company into receivership. However, he did not reckon on the public backlash that ensued. In making his calculations, he had failed to understand how deeply unpopular Railtrack's predecessor British Rail had been, nor had he appreciated the anger that the seizure of private property would provoke in the City of London, which demanded and eventually received financial compensation.

The Railtrack nationalisation is one of only a handful of examples (British Energy being another) of the state opting to take back control in the New Labour era. It was not a happy experience and in May 2002 it was the government that initially found itself in the firing line when an accident occurred at Potters Bar killing seven people and injuring 76 others. Railtrack was rapidly reorganised and underwent a name change, becoming Network Rail in October of the same year – a not-for-profit company controlled by an unwieldy board made up of all interested parties including consumer groups. Under the new regime, the safety of the system was improved by lavish investment in a modern, electronically controlled signalling system.

But while ownership of the infrastructure was brought back under state control, the rail franchises, which run on Network Rail's tracks, remained in private sector hands. Arriva was one British company that thrived in the environment created by privatisation. Traditionally a bus company, it came to run a large number of the nation's big city bus networks, including 20 per cent of London's routes. Not content with its British operations, it expanded successfully into Europe, buying coach, bus and train operations in the Netherlands, Germany and other markets as the Continent followed Britain in deregulating its transport networks. Indeed, by 2010, some 42 per cent of Arriva's profits and revenues were being earned in mainland Europe. While all this expansion was going on, it also bought the franchise to run Train Wales, later adding the CrossCountry rail network.

Arriva's reputation was such that it was even seen as a candidate to help bring some market-savvy reforms to the operations of the French railways SNCF as they are deregulated. But the chance never came along. The partly state-owned German railway Deutsche Bahn swooped in on Arriva in April 2010 and bought the company for £1.5 billion. The government chose not to intervene.

Commenting on the takeover, the *Daily Mail*'s veteran transport editor Ray Massey complained that Deutsche Bahn's raid marked 'the loss of yet another key element of Britain's manufacturing and infrastructure heritage to foreign ownership'. I also took a fairly dim view at the time:

The Deutsche Bahn bid has triumphed despite Lord Mandelson's promise of a 'Cadbury law' designed to toughen the scrutiny of takeovers to determine if they are in the 'public interest' and make it harder for foreign predators to snatch control of Britain's best companies. If nodded through by regulators in the UK and Germany it will be another blow to Britain's efforts to lead a free market revolution across Europe. A series of overseas bids for power and transport companies has shifted control of the privatised enterprises back into European state hands and made a mockery of the competitive model.

Furious unions condemned the takeover, saying that DB had 'slashed its workforce by half' since moves to privatise it began in 1994, and that the firm was 'aggressively raising capital' for further foreign takeovers as it sought to exploit liberalised European transport markets. The unions rightly feared that German domestic investment was most likely to be a higher priority than running the CrossCountry franchise or the unexciting local bus networks in cities such as Liverpool, Leeds, Leicester, Glasgow and Newcastle.

DB chief executive Rüdiger Grube sought to reassure the workforce and unions by saying that the Arriva brand was 'very, very valuable' and that the current headquarters would be maintained in Sunderland. He added that jobs were likely to be created rather than cut.

Arriva is not the only part of the transport network under foreign ownership. In fact the list of overseas companies is extensive. The Dutch government-owned Nederlandse Spoorwegen (NS) company used its German offshoot Abellio to partner service contractors Serco in a joint venture running Merseyrail services in and around Liverpool and Northern Rail across the north of England. The same Dutch firm also put in a bid to run the South Central franchise – which operates in London, Surrey, Sussex, Kent and Hampshire – under the name of NedRailways South Central.

In May 2009, it was announced that it was to buy Travel London, a bus operator, from National Express Group. In February 2011 foreign operators Deutsche Bahn, Spain's Renfe, Abellio and Italy's Trenitalia expressed interest in the profitable West Coast Main Line route operated by Virgin Trains.

Not all foreign takeovers of the transport network have been an unqualified success. Connex, for example, the French owners of the former British Rail Southern Region turned in a less than impressive performance when they had control of one of Britain's busiest commuter networks. Punctuality was appalling and the promised investment in new rolling stock never took place. The franchise, awarded in 1996, had originally been intended to run until 2011. But, in a highly unusual move in June 2003, the Strategic Rail Authority, one of the industry regulators, cut short the franchise, citing poor financial management and 'serious loss of confidence in the ability of the company to run the business in the widest sense'. Instead of bringing Continental efficiency to Britain, the new owners had seen the busy commuter business as a short cut to making profits. The resulting loss of the franchise is one of the few examples of overseas ownership being punished for its failure to run an enterprise in the best interest of its customers.

That said, superficially at least, privatisation, and the sell-off to foreign companies that has followed, has not been without its benefits. It has brought with it new investment in rolling stock, more choice and generally speaking better services to Britain's rail network.

Some would argue, of course, that other national train networks – France's in particular – are far more impressive. France was early to spot the value of building a north–south high-speed railway link, using government subsidy if necessary, to connect Paris to Lyon and beyond. Elsewhere, Germany's railways are renowned for their punctuality and cleanliness. Measured by customer convenience, reliability and the quality of investments made, French railways beat their British competitors hands down. And there was no greater emblem of the superiority of the French system of prioritising investment in infrastructure than the fast link to the Channel Tunnel. Paris's fast rail link to the tunnel opened almost simultaneously with the Chunnel in 1994. Embarrassingly, the Channel Tunnel Rail Link, known as High Speed 1, linking St Pancras in London to the entrance of the tunnel near Folkestone, was not opened until 13 years later.

The comparison, however, is not an entirely fair one. France's much-praised SNCF, which superficially operates at a profit, actually receives subsidies to the tune of €58 billion a year – or nearly 1 per cent of gross domestic product. The lobby group Transport Watch UK who have come up with this figure also note that a similar subsidy in the UK would require our spending £13 billion annually on our railways, or £520 for every household in the land. There is little willingness to make this kind of commitment, at either the electoral or government level.

That said, there are legitimate criticisms that can be made of the principle of foreign ownership of tracts of the British railway network. Leaving aside Connex's less than impressive performance, the fact is that while the train infrastructure may not receive the levels of public money that SNCF does, it is nevertheless subsidised. The annual subvention to the rail network, both Network Rail and train operating companies, reached £5 billion in 2009–2010. This might be considered a price worth paying for an efficient, safe, green and domestically owned and run train system.

But the reality is that with the arrival of foreign owners the British taxpayer is in effect subsidising the profits of foreign-owned franchises. So the hard-earned cash of ordinary British citizens is contributing to the profits and dividends of companies across Europe including state-controlled Deutsche Bahn in Germany. It is a bizarre outcome that has passed virtually unnoticed and cannot be considered an equitable or rational economic model.

The issue of exporting taxpayer funds to overseas investors will be writ large when the contracts for HS2, the high-speed railway linking London first to Birmingham and later to Manchester and the north, are let out by government. HS2 was signed off by the UK Conservative-led coalition government on 10 January 2012 with the tacit approval of the Labour opposition which had first developed the idea in government. Transport Secretary Justine Greening described the project as a 'good value for money project' and invoked the values of the Victorians who built Britain's first railways. The venture is one of the biggest infrastructure investments ever undertaken in Britain. The initial phase, the London to Birmingham route, will cost £16.3 billion. The eventual cost if the line is extended to Manchester and Leeds in 2032–2033 will be £37.2 billion. Government projections estimate that the potential benefit to the economy over 60 years will be £47 billion and the new railway will generate £34 billion of fares.

An infrastructure project on this scale could only be financed via government subsidy of one form or another, with the cost falling back on the taxpayer. Consequently, should the eventual train operators be chosen from overseas – as is already widely the case – British households will end up contributing to profits that will end up abroad.

No decisions have yet been taken and there are no clues as to the names of the engineering companies that will build the railways, the companies charged with building the high-speed trains, capable of running at 250 miles an hour, and the train operating companies which will run the new franchises. In the Victorian era there would have been no doubt. British engineers and train builders led the world. HS2 would offer British companies the chance to harness their inventive powers in research and development and new railway technology which, as in our Victorian past, could be exported to all corners of the earth. But if the contracts are awarded according to recent patterns, then there can be no guarantee that the enormous government resources applied to the project will flow back to British taxpayers. The UK's liberal approach to foreign ownership and involvement in our railways has, too often, worked against the broader public interest.

As questionable as allowing overseas companies to operate our train franchises is the wisdom of allowing so much expertise to be lost as control has moved abroad. Thanks to SNCF, France has developed successful train and coach manufacturers who have been able to compete for contracts as far away as Florida and California. Twenty or so years ago the same sort of claims could have been made for British manufacturers. In the 1980s and early 1990s, for example, the Anglo-French joint venture GEC Alsthom was regarded as a powerhouse of train making – among other things, it supplied the engines and coaches for Eurostar and the Seoul–Busan high-speed link in Korea. It was also the successful bidder, with Derby-based Bombardier, for Amtrak's prestigious high-speed Eastern Seaboard corridor linking Boston, New York and Washington.

But with the sale of GEC's share to Alstom, after the breakup of Lord (Arnold) Weinstock's empire in the early 1990s, UK production was run down and transferred to France. Local train manufacturing became a shadow of its former self. Just how far things had declined became apparent when the Conservative-led coalition government decided in June 2011 to award a £3 billion contract for new rolling stock for the Thameslink line to the German manufacturer Siemens. Bombardier, now a Canadian-owned firm, but Britain's last domestically centred train maker, was the loser. Bombardier revealed that 1,400 jobs would be lost and the future of train manufacture in this country looked to be threatened.

Transport Secretary Philip Hammond (who moved to the Ministry of Defence in October 2011) told the House of Commons that the decision had been taken by the Labour government a year earlier and had been settled strictly on the basis of European Commission rules which did not allow for national economic impact – such as the loss of jobs and supply chain – to be taken into account. The British mentality is to take EU directives at face value; the more general European mentality is to interpret them according to national interests. In explaining why Bombardier had lost out the UK government noted that Britain's European partners write their tenders for big infrastructure contracts taking note of social and domestic impacts in the home market.

In the wake of the Thameslink fiasco, Philip Hammond and Business Secretary Vince Cable wrote to Prime Minister David Cameron arguing that Britain – like its European partners – should take into account 'social factors', such as the impact on jobs and regions, in awarding future big contracts. But for Britain's once-thriving railway manufacturers, the intervention came far too late.

Airports and railways are, on a day-to-day basis, perhaps the most visible reminders of foreign involvement in Britain's transport infrastructure. But they are not the only parts of the transport system to have disappeared into foreign ownership. Various bridges, for example, are now no longer controlled by the country in which they were built. France's Cofiroute, part of the VINCI empire, holds the franchises to run some of Britain's most important bridges. It operates the Severn Bridge tolls and crossings which are part of the vital motorway network connecting England to South Wales. As for the Dartford Crossing, which carries M25 traffic between Kent and Essex, this was taken over in April 2003 by Le Crossing Company, in which France's Cofiroute and the UK's Babtie Group are partners.

UK-owned and controlled harbours and ports, both at home and across the world, have also fallen to overseas ownership. The surrender could not have come at a worse time, when international trade is so crucial to national prosperity.

Globalisation was neatly defined by the historian Niall Ferguson in his 2008 book *The Ascent of Money* as the 'rapid integration of international markets for commodities, manufactures, labour and money'. The principle is certainly nothing new: as Ferguson observes, in the three decades leading up to 1914 the trade in goods reached almost as large a proportion of global output as in the past 30 years. And Britain stood at the centre of the early twentieth-century globalisation with the London Stock Exchange listing the sovereign bonds of 57 different governments. British investment spread across the globe with 45 per cent to the Anglo-Saxon democracies, 20 per cent to Latin America, 16 per cent to Asia, 13 per cent to Africa and 6 per cent to the rest of Europe. Imperial Britain controlled the world's sea lanes and the ports.

Arguably, Britain's involvement goes back right to the pre-history of globalisation when, back in the twelfth century, a royal charter established the Cinque ports of Hastings, New Romney, Hythe, Dover and Sandwich to maintain ships for the Crown in case of need. In return, the five ports were granted exemption from taxes and tolls. The concept was so successful that it spread from the south-east to Liverpool, Bristol and London as overseas trade stepped up.

In the new age of globalisation trade volumes have again soared, capital has flowed across the continents and business and wealth has been more widely spread. Among the top 20 economies in the world, measured by gross domestic product, are the emerging markets of China, Russia, India, Mexico, South Korea, Turkey and Indonesia. Production in many cases has shifted from the high-cost Western economies to the cheaper Asian nations. World trade volumes have exploded along with logistics, shipping, container air freight and the transport links which connect ports and aeroports to warehouses, distribution centres and the big cities.

Yet, at a time when other maritime nations, such as China and the United Arab Emirates, are jealously guarding their own trading hubs and snapping up ports across the world, from Sri Lanka to Africa, Britain willingly sold off a great slug of the nation's infrastructure to the highest bidders – without any thought to the long-term impact of the disposals.

The great sell-off of British ports started in 2006 when buyers, including the investment bank Goldman Sachs, bought ownership of Associated British Ports (ABP) for £2.8 billion. ABP was a jewel in the crown of Britain's domestic transport and freight industry. More recently Forth Ports – the last remaining British port owner to be listed on the London Stock Exchange – was sold for £754 million in March 2011 to an assortment of financial groups (with the help of Germany's Deutsche Bank) led by a little-known European investment firm. The new company thus took control of London's Tilbury Docks, several Scottish ports and 400 acres of Edinburgh waterfront.

The most high-profile transaction in this sector was the takeover of P&O (Peninsular and Oriental Steam Navigation Company) – a company founded over 170 years earlier and with an unparalleled international infrastructure of container ports and ships. Under the captaincy of Jeffrey (later Lord) Sterling and his successors, P&O had cleverly spotted opportunities for container traffic as the world's manufacturing moved from Europe to Asia. It built up a network of ports across the Pacific and the Middle East to add to those it already controlled in Britain and the US. As trade rose so did freight rates and the opportunity for logistical, insurance and financial services tie-ins.

This success did not go unnoticed and the company was purchased in March 2006 by the United Arab Emirates state-owned company Dubai Ports World for $6.8 billion. Despite the oil riches of the Gulf region, this, like so many deals of the time, was one largely paid for with borrowed money. It came back to haunt Dubai later as the global economy staggered and the financial panic engendered by US sub-prime mortgages spread from the banking sector to the sovereign debt issued by states.

The consequence of all this short-sightedness by the get-rich-quick merchants in the City is that the UK no longer has a presence in a market that it once dominated. Much of this nation's imports and exports, from cars to raw material, pass through our ports, which are connected by rail terminals and haulage operations. Income is generated by container and terminal handling fees, shipping agencies, dredging and marine consultancy, not to mention financial services such as insurance. All that has passed beyond national control.

Does it matter? Many would argue not. In the spring of 2010, the Office of Fair Trading (OFT) began a review of British infrastructure, including ports, airports and energy networks. Its investigation was charged with looking at who controls what and to establish whether the consumer was being well served and competition kept open. It has to be said there was little political interest in the enterprise: it got going in the last months of New Labour's rule and was not seen as a priority for the Tory–Lib Dem coalition. Both David Cameron and Nick Clegg saw their main task as shrinking government after the spending binge of the Labour years, not in reviewing who owned which bits of the economy.

Nevertheless, the report was published in September 2010. Its conclusions were very mild. It concluded that foreign ownership was not necessarily a bad thing and suggested that overseas investment offered the chance to strengthen competition and drive down costs. Former Chancellor of the Exchequer Alistair Darling would concur. As Trade Secretary in the Blair administration in 2006 he declared:

> Whatever the short-term gains of protecting national industries, they are outweighed by the long-term costs. To retreat behind our borders and hope that barriers can keep the effects of globalisation at bay is a dangerous and ultimately ineffective option.

There are many economists who would agree with this prognosis. Tim Leunig of the London School of Economics, for example, takes a robust view of foreign ownership of much of Britain's electricity. 'It's not as if the French are turning off the electricity,' he argues, 'so what does it matter they are foreign owned? Neither French companies nor the French government have any incentive to do this. The commercial, legal and international ramifications would be enormous. And even if they decided they would, we could just turn it back on again.'

I am not convinced that a country's infrastructure is such a simple proposition. As Dieter Helm noted in the *Oxford Review of Economic Policy* in 2009, roads, railways, airports, broadband, electricity, gas and water and sewerage pipes are all fundamental to the functioning of any modern economy. Leaving aside the fact that they are essential to a nation's citizens, they also help give a country its competitive edge. High-quality, fast modern infrastructure acts as a magnet for both domestic and foreign investment. In the case of Britain, as an open trading economy, it is even more critical. Dissatisfaction with the capacity at the nation's airports might well, for example, lead investment banks to consider operating out of Frankfurt airport where there are more runways and more flexibility.

A 2012 study by the World Bank in Washington found that 'infrastructure helps determine the success of manufacturing and agricultural activities'. Investments in energy, sanitation, housing and transport improve lives and reduce poverty. And investments in new digital technologies improve the delivery of public services including education.

Moreover, whereas many companies can be allowed to fail if they fall on hard times, infrastructure needs constant support. It also needs high levels of investment. In the period 2005–2010 an estimated £150 billion was invested in new basic facilities in the UK – and many would argue that it was insufficient. Some estimates suggest that another £500 billion of investment will be needed over the next ten years – a massive undertaking, and a task that will ultimately be paid for by those living in the UK. While privatisation has proved beneficial in many ways, unbridled privatisation and foreign ownership has already been shown to have its weaknesses and poses risks for the country in the years ahead.

Infrastructure also needs to be accountable. Consider, for

example, the tortuous chain of ownership now involved in Associated British Ports, the largest UK ports operator, which handles a quarter of the nation's seaborne trade from 21 domestic facilities. ABP began life as the British Transport Docks Board in 1962, was privatised by the Thatcher government in 1982 and over the decades has been the subject of various bid approaches.

In July 2006 the regulators cleared a foreign consortium £3.17 billion takeover bid. The consortium was led by US bankers Goldman Sachs which proposed a £2.85 billion buyout. Goldman Sachs dropped out after allegations of a conflict of interests between its role as adviser to ABP and potential buyer of the company. Consequently in 2006, ABP, now controlled from Jersey (outside British tax jurisdiction), was sold to a consortium made up of a Canadian pensions fund and propped up by a Goldman Sachs infrastructure investment fund. With the sale went 21 of the nation's key ports including Southampton, Plymouth, Cardiff and Immingham on the east coast. Such at-a-distance control scarcely inspires confidence.

Not only does infrastructure need to be accountable, it also needs to be clearly aligned with the national interest. The nation's biggest container port Felixstowe was bought by billionaire Li Ka-shing's Hong Kong-based trading empire Hutchison Whampoa back in 1991. At one level, it has enjoyed heavy inward investment by its overseas owners. But the considerable income and profits that have flowed in have been repatriated overseas and instead of becoming an international hub for Britain – with all the capacity the country has to exploit the globalisation of trade – it has effectively become an outpost of Hong Kong. At a time when international trade is booming and new naval powers like China are moving in for the kill, developing new ports and trade routes across the globe from Colombo in Sri Lanka to Lagos in Nigeria,

Britain's ports lack an overall national strategy and serve foreign masters.

If nothing else, policymakers ought to be concerned that a path that the British have been so happy to go along has not been adopted in a similarly enthusiastic way by other countries. As I have already pointed out, several key utilities have been taken over not by private companies, but by companies with broader supernational ambitions. When Paris-based EDF became involved in Britain's electricity supply, it was not as a stateless organisation but as a French power company seeking to extend its grasp. Similarly when Dubai Ports World bought P&O, this was a major trading nation buying into Britain's mercantile power.

Interestingly, the Dubai Ports World deal caused consternation in the US where then Senator Hillary Clinton argued powerfully that it was against the national interest. It was one thing when Eastern Seaboard ports were controlled by Britain – after all, the two countries enjoyed a 'special' strategic relationship. It was quite another when the new owner was a state from a part of the world which had, at best, an uneasy relationship with America.

As a result of the US outcry, which went as high as the White House, the sale of the six P&O ports in North America was restructured so that they remained under US control. It may have seemed ironic to many that of all people it should be the Americans – champions of global capitalism – who had baulked at the eleventh hour. But they clearly felt that their strategic interests were under threat. In point of fact, their move ultimately proved to have economic wisdom behind it too when Dubai later found itself in the embarrassing position of being unable to pay its bills.

Dubai's debt-ridden investments should give cause for concern, and they are not unique. The financial free-for-all of the past few years has essentially been funded by unstable debt. The very openness of capital markets has allowed the build-up of enormous imbalances between surplus nations like China, Japan, Korea and Germany and deficit countries like Britain and the US. Overseas companies have queued up to acquire British assets on financial bases that are far from secure. Hunger for quick returns and the need to service debt is not the best combination for companies running vital and long-term infrastructure. And governments that pretend that, for the purposes of foreign ownership, little will change on the international scene in the future are foolish in the extreme.

Lord Sterling, one of Mrs Thatcher's most admired businessmen who helped rebuild P&O into a global shipping, container and ports giant, and who was the first head of the joint Lords and Commons National Security Strategy Committee set up in May 2010, laments the lack of long-term thinking. When I interviewed him in his well-appointed offices in Mayfair, he told me that in his corporate days he would have taken a 50-year view, but that he could think of no recent example where, say, the Foreign Office would engage in long-term modelling in terms of the impact of a particular decision on Britain's economic future. Such a short-term mentality is worrying.

8

The Wealth Funds are Coming

It was a fine spring day in London in May 2009 when a cavalcade of bulletproof limousines, complete with burly bodyguards in dark suits and sporting sunglasses and security earpieces, pulled into the courtyard of the Prince of Wales's residence, Clarence House, just off The Mall. Officially, the Emir of Qatar, Sheikh Hamad bin Khalifa Al Thani, his glamorous second wife Sheikha Mozah and closest advisers were in Britain on business to open a gas terminal in Wales. Unofficially, they had agreed to come to the Prince's official home, at his request, to discuss another matter altogether.

Charles was deeply concerned about redevelopment plans for the 12-acre former Chelsea Barracks site. The site – one of the most valuable in London, adjacent to the King's Road and a stone's throw from the Thames – was in the final stages of preparation for major construction. And the funding was coming from Qatar.

The property had been bought by residential tycoon Christian Candy and his brother in conjunction with the state-backed Qatari Diar consortium for £959 million in 2007. Architect Lord (Richard) Rogers had then been invited to come up with designs to transform the site into 548 glass-and-concrete luxury apartments for the rich and famous. But Prince Charles, quite simply, hated what was planned. He called Rogers's scheme 'one more brutalist development' and in March 2009 wrote to Qatar's prime minister, cousin of the Emir and chairman of Qatari Diar, to express his concerns. It later emerged that the Prince's letter stated, among other things: 'It is a site of great importance – I can only urge you to reconsider the plans.'

At the meeting at Clarence House, the Prince repeated his concerns. He found he was pushing at an open door. Some have suggested that part of the reason for this was that he had similar charity interests to Sheikha Mozah and this had placed them on friendly terms. Doubtless, too, the Emir did not want in any way to jeopardise his excellent relations with the British royal family. After all, Sheikh Hamad bin Khalifa Al Thani's visit to the UK had opened with a spectacular horse-drawn carriage procession to Windsor Castle where he and his wife were entertained in grand style by the Queen and Prince Philip. Within a month, the planning application for the glass-and-steel towers had been withdrawn.

The Candy brothers and Rogers were incensed and a court case ensued. In May 2010 the matter went to the High Court in London. It was alleged that the Qatari royal family had made a private deal with the Prince, and the Candy brothers' CPC Group sued Qatari Diar for the £81 million it would have been paid had planning consent been given. In a ruling in June 2010 Mr Justice Vos found that the Qatari partners had breached the terms of their agreement after the intervention of the Prince of Wales. But he also ruled that the Candy company, CPC group, was not entitled to a payout of £68.5 million as specified in the original contract.

The whole affair reveals nothing new about architectural debate in the UK – after all, Prince Charles's views on modern architecture are well known. But it does provide a brief, sideways glimpse at the secretive world – and the immense financial power – of the sovereign wealth fund.

Essentially, sovereign wealth funds (SWFs) were born of high oil prices. In the wake of the 1967 six-day war, the 1973 Yom Kippur war and the Iranian revolution, the balance of financial power shifted massively from the oil-consuming states to the oil producers. These suddenly found petro-dollars flooding in at a greater rate than they could absorb, and the result was the establishment of SWFs as a form of long-term savings, designed to ensure that some of the wealth was preserved for the day the oil and gas reserves might have run out.

Historically, the funds were regarded as 'passive' investors – a bit like trust funds. Essentially, they safeguarded their assets for the long term, rather than adopting the role of 'active' investors, trading in and out of shares, property and other assets. But over the decades they have become much more vigorous and much less predictable in their behaviour.

Qatar offers a good example of sovereign wealth funds in action. Within a matter of a few years, the country has been transformed from being one of the poorest Gulf statelets – a backward autocracy dependent on pearl fishing for its income – to becoming the second richest nation on earth (measured by head of population). Much of the reason for this is that it is, quite simply, blessed with oil. It has proven reserves of 15 billion barrels which, according to estimates by America's intelligence agency the CIA, should last another 37 years at current extraction rates. That quantity is probably enough to keep this small country, with a labour force of just over 1 million, going for decades if not centuries to come.

However, what makes Qatar really different, as one well-placed City of London source says, is that it 'floats on a sea of natural gas'. The resources controlled by Sheikh Hamad are truly breathtaking. CIA data shows that it has 25 trillion cubic metres [a trillion is

1,000 billion] of natural gas beneath its sandy wastes. This is sufficient to supply 14 per cent of the world's demand for natural gas
and represents the third largest stock of natural gas on the planet.

Indeed, amid fears that the unusually severe winter of 2010 was
placing an almost insupportable strain on energy supplies in the
UK, the Sheikh was able to come to the rescue straight away with
emergency supplies. At the peak of the potential crisis Qatar was
providing 10 per cent of Britain's energy needs.

The current Emir seized power from his father in 1995 after the
economy had been undermined by the elder Al Thani's extrava-
gant lifestyle. Sheikh Hamad, the younger Al Thani, proved to be
very different. A senior British executive with extensive dealings
with the Qataris says that these days they are determined to turn
the nation's gas assets into 'long-term investments and have hired
professional managers to handle the transition'.

By the standards of the region, Qatar's ruler is a relative liberal,
opening the affairs of the region to detailed TV scrutiny through
the Western-style Al Jazeera satellite service. The 1999 municipal
elections were the first in the region in which Qatari women were
allowed to vote and in the past decade there has been further
democratic reform. It is a country able to straddle the very
different mores of East and West. 'When you travel to Qatar to
pursue a deal,' one insider says, 'you are whisked off to a waiting
area and promised a meeting with the decision-maker (usually the
prime minister) shortly. Then you are kept hanging around for
several hours, without any word of when the audience will take
place. You are then shuffled into a room filled with men in long
white robes and keffiyeh. These were the very same people,' he
adds, 'who just a few weeks earlier had been in your office in
immaculate Savile Row suits and talked the language of the
Harvard Business School.'

The Sheikh's sovereign fund has amassed $54 billion. And the Emir has proved himself a shrewd investor. He chooses his targets carefully. His technique, and that of his advisers, is generally to be 'invited in' rather than blundering in unsupported. Aside from acquiring a stake in Barclays and the London Stock Exchange, he has gravitated toward the capital's prime real estate market. Without Qatar's backing, the Candy & Candy development at One Hyde Park, one of London's best addresses, would almost certainly have been halted by the worst financial meltdown since the Great Depression. It was no surprise then when Qatar's foreign minister (another member of the ruling clan) stepped in to pay £100 million for a penthouse apartment, setting a very high bar for the rest of the development.

Today, from One Hyde Park to the hole in the ground which was once the prestigious Chelsea Barracks, Qatar holds some of the most valuable real estate in Britain. Just to underline its continuing interest, in July 2011 – with a year to go to the 2012 London Olympics – Qatari Diar revealed it was linking with property group Delancey Estates (vehicle of the Ritblat family) to buy the Olympic site in Stratford, East London. At the same time, it also bought the largest development site to become available on Oxford Street in decades, purchasing a large stretch of land close to Marble Arch from the British property giant Land Securities for £250 million. In addition, the Sheikh has paid almost £1 billion for the Grosvenor Square home of the American Embassy, which is scheduled to become a fancy hotel.

Among his latest targets is thought to be the auction house Christie's. When he was in Britain visiting the Queen, he remarked to an enquirer: 'Thank you for reminding me about Christie's.' But Qatar has not confined itself to trophy holdings in West London. In 2010, on the other side of town, it became the biggest investor in Canary Wharf – London's 'Wall Street by the river' – home to all the major investment banks. It is also the financier behind the City's tallest tower, known as the Shard of Glass, at London Bridge.

Among its most sensitive holdings is a stake in the supermarket group J. Sainsbury. As the founding Sainsbury family has loosened its grip on the business, the Qataris have enlarged their share. They currently control 25.93 per cent of the supermarket group and there is regular speculation that, the Sainsbury family permitting, the Sheikh would like the lot.

The Gulf states control perhaps the best-known SWFs – the Kuwait Investment Authority, for example, has been around since the 1950s and famously took a 22 per cent stake in BP in 1988. But they are not the only ones. Another early subscriber to the club was Norway. As oil and gas flowed from the North Sea in the 1980s and beyond, it took the decision not to follow what Britain had done and use oil revenues to bolster the national finances in the short term, but to save for the future.

It has now built up a £300 billion pension investment fund, designed to ensure future old-age provision for the whole of the country's population. Managed by the country's Norges Bank, it insists on ethical investment and has a long blacklist, which includes tobacco companies such as Britain's BAT, and various American military contractors. Occasionally that ethical imperative can have a political slant to it. For example, the fund took the decision to disinvest from Israel's Elbit Systems, an advanced technology firm, because it had been involved in supplying surveillance systems along Israel's security fence with the Palestinian West Bank.

Nor are oil rich countries the only ones to have SWFs. By 2011, there were an estimated 50 major sovereign funds worldwide representing all continents, and each reported to have up to

£600 billion available to invest. Based on estimated cash holdings, the leading players include: Abu Dhabi Investment Authority (United Arab Emirates); Government Pension Fund (Norway); SAMA Foreign Holdings (Saudi Arabia); SAFE Investment Company and HKMA (both China); Singapore Investment Corporation and Kuwait Investment Authority. Not counted among these are some of the state pension funds of G7 allies such as the US and Canada, which are big investors in Britain and around the world.

Not every SWF has been a glittering success. Dubai, the shining star of the Gulf region, fell prey to the allure of over-accelerated expansion and so became one of the first nations to be caught up in a sovereign debt crisis. On 26 November 2010, Dubai World, the investment vehicle for the emirate and a semi-official company encouraged by the ruling Al Maktoum family, proposed delaying repayment of its debt, which raised the risk of the largest government default since the Argentine debt restructuring in 2001. It sought a six-month delay in payment on £18 billion of debt with 70 creditors facing write-downs.

Nevertheless, the sums of cash most of these countries have to spend are eye-watering. Thanks largely to the energy sector, Russia earns around £500 million a day from exports and its stabilisation fund is expected to grow by £25 billion a year. Saudi Arabia takes in over £300 million. Such income means that countries with external surpluses are accumulating vast foreign exchange reserves which, in China's case, are estimated at $3 trillion. China Investment is projected to grow by £140 billion a year. Similarly placed are other Far-Eastern states including Singapore, Malaysia and South Korea. At one point Merrill Lynch analysts were predicting that capital managed by the funds could hit nearly $8 trillion by 2011.

Worries about very heavy investment by one country in another are nothing new. Back in 1992 Michael Crichton's popular novel *Rising Sun*, later a Hollywood blockbuster, expressed a widely felt American concern at Japan's direct investment in America's high-technology industries and the potential for a transfer of skills and business to Japan that might ultimately entail. Certainly, the figures gave pause for thought: at the start of the 1980s, Japan's investment in the US was a modest $8.7 billion. By 1990, it had grown to $83.1 billion. However, relative to the overall size of the US economy, Japanese investment was modest, and some felt that the debate round the book and film acquired an unpleasantly racist overtone. *New York Times* critic Christopher Lehmann-Haupt concluded: 'The trouble with *Rising Sun* is obviously that as a serious discourse on why we should begin waging economic war against Japan, the book is far too entertaining. And as an entertainment, it is far too didactic.'

The issue, then, is not whether SWFs should be allowed to invest in other countries, but the extent to which their investment should be permitted. Is there, in other words, a point at which the host nation weakens itself by allowing so much of its national wealth to be under the control of others? And can certain SWFs be regarded as a potential national threat? No one suggested in the 1990s that Japan and the US were on anything but friendly terms, even though they may have been economic rivals. But not all nations with sovereign wealth funds can be said to be similarly well disposed. Consequently, when considering whether the sell-off of Britain's assets to foreign buyers has been beneficial or not, the role of SWFs cannot be ignored.

Take China, for example. Such has been its economic rise that it now wields huge financial muscle, and it has a stake in many countries around the world. Its extensive investments in Africa have brought with them enormous control over valuable mineral deposits. Its investments in other parts of Asia have brought it control of key raw products, such as rubber (which is now extensively farmed in countries such as Laos). No one could claim, however, that it has been traditionally regarded as a close ally of the West – nor that its heavy investments in Africa and elsewhere have automatically brought benefits to any country other than China.

It's perhaps not surprising therefore that when China's state-owned National Offshore Oil Corporation – a wealth fund specialising in oil assets – made an $18.5 billion bid for the US oil conglomerate Unocal in 2005, the move provoked outrage on Capitol Hill. Joe Barton, the Republican chairman of the House Energy and Commerce Committee, wrote to the president to demand the deal be halted. 'The Chinese are great economic and political rivals, not friendly competitors or allies in democracy,' he insisted. The language was carefully chosen. During his 2000 election campaign, George W. Bush had declared China to be 'a strategic competitor'.

In the end, the deal went for review to the Committee on Foreign Investment (CFIUS), under the auspices of the US Treasury, which turned it down on national security grounds. In 1999 the same committee had rejected the sale to a Chinese consortium of the bankrupt telecoms company Global Crossing on the same grounds. It did, however, allow the sale of IBM's personal computing arm to Chinese competitor Lenovo.

Russian investment in other countries has similarly caused concern in some quarters. The actions of Russia's state-owned gas company Gazprom exemplify how state-owned enterprises can be used to achieve political objectives. The head of Gazprom publicly threatened the EU that it would divert supplies from Europe if Gazprom's plans to enter the European market were thwarted. This can hardly be viewed as an idle threat, given Russia's willingness to use its power in the natural gas market as weapons against Ukraine in 2005–2006 and 2009 and in Georgia in 2007. As the price of natural gas soared, there were brown-outs of power across Europe, and Britain, at the end of the pipeline, faced power cuts.

And the Russians are certainly coming. Vneshtorgbank, a Russian state-owned bank, has built up a 5 per cent stake in the European Aeronautic Defence and Space Company (EADS), the European aerospace consortium. In addition to the Vneshtorgbank, other Russian investors are interested in taking a massive share in EADS.

Part of the problem is, of course, that relations with other countries are inevitably unpredictable. A thaw at one point – as happened between Russia and the West in the late 1980s and 1990s – can very easily turn frosty again. The deal that seemed so good at the time becomes an embarrassment – or worse – a few years later. Libya affords a salutary tale. A pariah state for many years, it was to some extent rehabilitated in the early years of the twenty-first century. Then the Arab Spring occurred, leading to the collapse of Colonel Gaddafi's Libyan regime in August 2011.

The Libyan Investment Authority, with funds of an estimated $70 billion, was established in 2006 by Gaddafi's son Saif al-Islam, the controversial PhD alumnus of the London School of Economics. It had stakes in the Italian bank UniCredit, in Pearson, publisher of the *Financial Times*, and in the Italian soccer club Juventus, among others. Following the collapse of the regime, allegations were made that funds were missing and the new government in Libya indicated it might want to repatriate funds to help improve infrastructure at home.

Concern has also been voiced about the comparatively secret way in which SWFs operate. In political terms, it can never be precisely known what the agenda is of the controlling country, nor indeed who precisely is running the fund. In the case of Singapore's Temasek the fund was run until October 2009, by Ho Ching, wife of Prime Minister Lee Hsien Loong (after that an outside chairman, Charles Goodyear of the British-based mining giant BHP Billiton, was appointed). It is hard to imagine that in a state like Singapore, where power is so concentrated, the strategic and political interests of the sovereign fund and the nation were likely to diverge – especially when there was a husband-and-wife team in charge. In China it is almost impossible to separate the big state enterprises, which make many of the large investments, from the decision-making central committee of the PRC itself. As for Russia, it has used several shell companies operating in Cyprus to undertake transactions. In other words, the danger always exists that countries use their SWFs as an extension of their foreign policy or to pursue broader economic interests other than preserving or creating new wealth for their population or boosting investment returns.

This all goes hand in hand with a tendency, as in private equity, to keep disclosure to a minimum. Few of the sovereign funds publish their management structures or investment objectives. Dubai World even threatened to pull out of investing in Europe in March 2008, when the EU sought to impose on it rules for governance and objectives. As I wrote in my *Mail* column:

> There has been concern for some time about the lack of transparency and weak governance in Sovereign Wealth Funds. Now we understand why.

On occasion SWFs have even acted without first consulting the company in which they have invested. In June 2009, for example,

Abu Dhabi's International Petroleum Investment Company sold £3.5 billion worth of Barclays shares, without warning, for a speedy profit of £1.5 billion. It was a move that sent the shares of the bank spinning.

It's not surprising, then, that many countries regard SWFs with a degree of caution. EU fears escalated sharply after China let it be known that it would deploy £120 billion of its vast foreign reserves through the new state-controlled vehicle, the China Investment Company. In 2011, Peer Steinbrück, Germany's Finance Minister, indicated that his country was looking to draw up detailed plans to shield companies in strategic sectors – such as telecoms, banks, communications, logistics and energy – from takeover by funds such as China's, as well as by some 'private finance houses'.

Germany's coalition government head, Chancellor Angela Merkel, has come out in favour of a collective EU vetting policy on overseas state-backed investors. She herself blocked Russia's Mischkonzerns Sistema attempt to invest in Deutsche Telekom, the largest communications company in Europe, in November 2007. As for French President Nicolas Sarkozy, he has demanded that Brussels competition watchdogs bend tough rules on state aid to allow governments to take stakes in key industries, protecting companies from non-European takeovers. Such has the concern of individual EU countries been, that the European Commission has undertaken its own investigation to ascertain whether takeovers by publicly controlled foreign investment funds threaten Europe's capital market.

Britain, by contrast, has adopted a very relaxed approach. A 12.7 per cent stake in Britain's Gatwick Airport went to the California Public Employees' Retirement System (CalPERS) in 2009, when BAA owner Ferrovial sold it off for £1.5 billion. In March 2010 the National Lottery – an institution as British as it could be with its funds spent in good causes from the arts to the 2012 London Olympics – went to the Ontario Teachers State Pension Fund for £385 million. As usual, the change of ownership, from a consortium of UK companies including Cadbury (now owned by Kraft Foods) and banknote printer De La Rue, barely raised an eyebrow among politicians or the media.

Singaporean fund Temasek bought a large 12 per cent stake in Standard Chartered Bank in 2006, topping up its holding to 18.8 per cent in early 2008. The keen interest of Temasek in Standard Chartered is not that surprising given the bank's strong roots in the Far East and its decision to locate large-scale operations in Singapore as well as Hong Kong.

In the build-up to the financial crisis, sovereign funds were as busy as other overseas investors in increasing their exposure to Britain. In June and July 2007, just before financial markets froze over, Singapore funds bought a property group that owns Merrill Lynch Financial Centre in London for around £800 million. It took a 50 per cent stake in the WestQuay shopping centre in Southampton for about £500 million and invested over £1 billion in Barclays. In September, Dubai and Qatar funds bought their hefty stakes in the London Stock Exchange.

In the autumn of 2008 Barclays announced that it had arranged an injection of £4.5 billion ($8.8 billion) in new capital from overseas investors. The biggest investor was the Qatar Investment Authority, which contributed £1.7 billion, giving it a whopping 7.7 per cent share of the business. A separate Qatari company Challenger, owned directly by the company's ruler Sheikh Hamad bin Jassim bin Jabr Al Thani invested £533 million in the business. Temasek, the Singapore wealth fund, increased its stake to 2.9 per cent and the state-controlled China Development Bank moved its holding up to 3.1 per cent.

And Norway has bought into the UK too. The £400 billion Norwegian fund, the world's second biggest pension fund, bought a quarter of London's Regent Street, after receiving government approval to invest 5 per cent of its portfolio in real estate over the first half of 2011.

It's Britain's short-termist view, its willingness to grab any deal going without investigation that is so worrying. Many of the deals in themselves make complete sense. In the case of the London Stock Exchange, for example, Dubai and Qatar acted as 'white knights' buying share stakes to keep the LSE independent and out of the hands of overseas rivals. After the credit crunch, sovereign funds played a big role in the recapitalisation of Britain's banks, most notably Barclays. But as the SWFs become more powerful and the balance of economic power shifts ever further from the developed to the developing world, the lack of scrutiny becomes a matter for evermore concern. And, in the case of countries such as Russia or China, there has been a strategic concern that their national funds are acting as Trojan horses that enable mercantilist states to muscle in on free market economies.

Some critics see the funds as a threat to the very sovereignty of the nations in whose corporations they invest. There are also concerns that foreign government funds are enabling the distinction between private and state involvement to be blurred with the governments simply masquerading as free market corporations. In the case of funds of some of the world's less open countries the concern is that these nations are seeking to gain political influence by the back door.

And it's as well to remember just how indebted some developed nations are now becoming to other countries. US debt in the hands of foreign governments, for instance, stood at 25 per cent of the total in 2007, compared with 13 per cent in 1988. At the end of 2006, non-US citizens and institutions held 44 per cent of federal debt held by the public. About 66 per cent of that was held by the central banks of other countries, in particular those of Japan and China. By May 2009, the US owed China $772 billion.

Such a state of affairs inevitably exposes America to potential financial or political risk should foreign banks stop buying Treasury securities or start selling them heavily. This was clearly spelled out in a series of reports from 2009 to 2011 by the influential Basel-based Bank for International Settlements:

> Foreign investors in US dollar assets have seen big losses measured in dollars, and still bigger ones measured in their own currency. While unlikely, indeed highly improbable for public sector investors, a sudden rush for the exits cannot be ruled out completely.

With the global imbalances accumulated over the past decade or so, it has become apparent that sovereign funds could be the new acquisition masters taking over from highly leveraged private equity titans. Strong global growth has brought a striking increase in the foreign currency receipts of many energy and commodity-exporting economies. Effective wealth management has become an important public sector responsibility and many countries have responded by creating funds.

The funds of tomorrow are likely to be more interested – in Russia's case – in strategic companies with high-tech capabilities or techniques. The Russians are after significant industrial assets. The Kremlin's £80 billion Stabilisation Fund, which represents about 10 per cent of the country's GDP, made a profit of £2.8 billion in 2007. Simultaneously, the Chinese, along with managing their huge trade surpluses and vast reserves of foreign exchange, are seeking access to emerging markets and to continents with the natural resources needed for their booming industrial economy. 'Their investments are not purely commercial or about maximising the value of their portfolio,' said Jan Randolph, head of Sovereign Risk at Global Insight. 'They're looking at ways of developing their economies.'

How the funds decide to invest their vast pile of cash will play a pivotal role in reshaping financial markets in the next decade. Funds are going to have the ability to buy any global company, to create panic in markets if they move too precipitously, even to dwarf the political clout of international financial institutions. Many countries are aware of this. Britain, so far, has turned a blind eye.

9

Living with the Consequences

I am keeping a weather eye on this area because I have started to become concerned that over a lengthy period of time . . . UK manufacturing could be a loser.

Lord Mandelson's comment to the *Wall Street Journal* in September 2009, as Kraft Foods began its pursuit of Cadbury, is one of the very few made by politicians in recent years that accepts that foreign takeovers might not always be in the national interest. Mandelson set out his stall very clearly, arguing that as a 'general rule' markets should remain open to foreign takeovers, but that Britain needed to be 'mindful' of the long-term effects of foreign ownership.

By March 2010 – with Kraft completing the deal – Mandelson's stance had toughened:

It is hard to ignore the fact that the fate of a company [Cadbury] with a long history and many tens of thousands of employees was decided by people who had not owned the company a few weeks before and who had no intention of owning it a few weeks later.

He now argued that board directors should consider the interests of all stakeholders in a business: employees, suppliers, company brands and capabilities. They should act more like stewards and less like auctioneers. But his words fell on deaf ears. When push came to shove, Mandelson was powerless to act. Up until 2002 he might have been able to counter such a takeover by assuming ministerial responsibility to prevent an action that could be said to harm the 'economic interests of consumers'. Thanks to the 2002 Enterprise Act, however, that leverage had gone. Now the power to step in rested in professionals at the Office of Fair Trading and Competition Commission who could only operate in a very circumscribed way. In the final days of New Labour vague promises to review foreign bids were made and new rules mooted for policing takeovers. Nothing happened.

Former Cadbury chairman and president of the CBI Sir Roger Carr laments this apparent powerlessness. In conversation with me at the headquarters of Centrica he said:

> At the moment we have a public interest test which is pretty much focused on military issues, so it is Rolls-Royce and BAE. It doesn't go much beyond that. If I were in government I might look to have an instrument that I could use, and use on a broader front than simply military issues, if I felt it was appropriate . . . I think what you don't want is to make noise from the sidelines with no ability to affect the outcome.

Up until – and, indeed, after – the Kraft–Cadbury affair, New Labour took a very relaxed view of foreign takeovers – far more relaxed, certainly, than Britain's competitors. This is reflected in the figures. Data produced by the Paris-based economic monitor the OECD shows that in each of the years 2006 to 2010 foreign investment in British stocks and shares exceeded a trillion US dollars a year, reaching $1.2 trillion in 2010. This far exceeded the $910 billion flowing into the much larger German economy in the same year and the $214 billion into Japan. Only the United States, a far bigger economy, attracted greater overseas investment, in its stocks and shares. Between 1997 and 2007, in fact, according to Treasury analysis, foreign ownership rose from 30 to 50 per cent of national output.

As a percentage of gross domestic product (the total output of the economy) overall foreign direct investment in the UK was an enormous 6.4 per cent in 2006, the peak of the financial boom, against just 1.9 per cent in Germany, 1.8 per cent in the United States and 0.5 per cent in Japan. Even as financial flows were cut back in the period 2008–2010 the UK was by far the most popular destination for foreign takeovers and investment.

In the years 2005 to 2008 cross-border mergers in the UK represented close to 50 per cent of those across the whole European Union – the biggest economic bloc in the world.

As the full force of the financial downturn hit the global economy, the momentum briefly slowed, but by 2010 it was business as normal, with the UK selling companies worth $58 billion against $113 billion for the whole of the rest of the EU. Judging from current trends, only a lack of acquisition targets could potentially slow the momentum – and, given the scale of Britain's sell-offs, that could well happen sooner rather than later.

Until the economic crisis of 2007–2008 the worst effects of the British approach were hidden by the strength of its banking and services sector. As the manufacturing share of the economy shrank to just 12.4 per cent in 2007 (compared with 29 per cent in Germany), so the banking and financial sector became more important. In the 1950s it had represented just 2 per cent of gross domestic product. By the time the credit crunch arrived in 2007 it accounted for 10 per cent of GDP. If other finance-related services, including accounting, law, management consulting and IT, are added, the figure could be as high as 30 per cent. As things currently stand, the largest sector of the economy is services, which amount to 73 per cent of GDP if ancillary services (some of which overlap with those called upon by the financial sector) are taken into account.

But the banking crisis revealed the fragility of an economy so heavily dependent on this now volatile sector. And the sheer scale of the banking bail-out required made Britain's decision to forsake manufacturing in favour of finance look like a very bad deal. A report by the accountants PwC for the City of London found that in the peak year of 2007, running up to the banking crisis, the Square Mile generated £67.8 billion of taxes for the government. That sum is, however, dwarfed by the £1 trillion of rescue funds that Gordon Brown's government poured into the banking system in September 2011 in the wake of the collapse of American investment bankers Lehman Brothers.

What's more, the lack of a vibrant manufacturing base was now shown to be impeding economic recovery – a state of affairs that will continue to operate well into the future. In previous decades, British manufacturing has shown amazing resilience in times of economic hardship. John Major's 'accidental' devaluation of 1992, for example, which came about when Britain fell out of the exchange rate mechanism (the precursor of the eurozone) was followed by an unprecedented boom. The same happened after devaluations in 1967 and in 1976. In all cases, the UK was able to take advantage of a cheaper currency to build its exports.

And the same happened in 2010–2011 following the 20 per cent fall in sterling against a basket of currencies of our major trading partners. Among car manufacturers, for instance, a notable pick up in the volume of exports became apparent. The transformed overseas-owned Jaguar Land Rover, Nissan and Toyota all benefited, finding themselves in the position of being able to export four out of every five cars sold. Early in 2012 Rolls-Royce motor cars (owned by BMW) reported a 31 per cent lift in sales to a historic record of 3,538. In a completely different sector, British-owned Burberry reported in early 2012 that sales had jumped by 21 per cent, helped in part by the growth of the Chinese market.

But the problem this time has been that there simply has not been enough of a manufacturing base to give the economy as a whole the support it needs. What's more, those manufacturers that are still going strong often have to import key components from overseas because so much of the supply chain has been fractured, so diluting the benefits of any uplift in export sales yet further. It's worth bearing in mind in this context that one of the reasons why Derby-based Bombardier lost out to Siemens on the Thameslink train system contract was the dearth of local suppliers of vital component parts. Sir James Dyson, for his part, has stated that the lack of British-made components were a major consideration when he made the decision to move manufacturing of his goods overseas. In an interview with the *Daily Mail* in August 2011 he pulled no punches:

The supply chain just vanished in Britain in the eighties and nineties. When we were manufacturing here, we found that our manufacturers didn't actually want us to expand, because they didn't want the risk of taking on more people and bigger premises. We have had an anti-entrepreneurial system that has totally wrecked our supply chain. I used to be able to go to Birmingham and find all the components I needed. Now I have to go to Taiwan in order to make a British plug.

New Labour had a hands-off approach to global capitalism in general, and foreign takeovers in particular. There's no suggestion that the coalition government under Cameron and Clegg are thinking very differently. Amid the dozens of inquiries which the government has conducted into everything from the failings of the press to the fall of the Royal Bank of Scotland to the Leveson Inquiry into the press, none has been commissioned to look at the reshaping of commerce in the UK.

In terms of economic policy, the coalition government took the view that deleveraging the British economy, by shrinking the size of the state, was the first priority. It was only when growth began to stall in 2011 – after a sharp rise in energy prices and the breakdown of budgetary discipline in the eurozone – that refloating the economy became part of the agenda.

Seeking to define a new national economic agenda Chancellor George Osborne used his March 2011 Budget speech to promise a 'March of the Makers'. There then followed various schemes to encourage manufacturing and entrepreneurship. Small and medium-sized enterprises, however, have consistently reported that it is proving very difficult to obtain the necessary financing to expand, so it is not exactly surprising that signs of the promised manufacturing renaissance are proving singularly difficult to spot.

The consequence of all this is that Britain's economy now resembles a jigsaw puzzle that has seen happier days. Originally, all the pieces were there, but then the children – or, rather, politicians, financiers and others – thoughtlessly mislaid many of them. Some remain, bearing images of pharmaceutical, car assembly and aerospace companies and services from finance to architecture. But there are great jagged gaps too.

So bad has the problem become that it now extends beyond manufacturing to the creative industries. Together, these sectors, which extend from literature to music, and from computer software to console 'game' design and costume drama, accounted for as much as 10 per cent of the economy in 2011 – almost as much as finance. Music was a particular strength, as the country that produced Elgar and the Beatles was also at the cutting edge of producing new artistes including the late Amy Winehouse, Leona Lewis and Adele, all products of the Brit School in unfashionable Croydon.

But when in 2011 Britain's largest record producer EMI was put up for sale by its owners Citigroup – which had taken control from the British private equity firm Terra Firma – there was no UK buyer in the wings nor any attempt by Whitehall or government to see if a British solution to its future could be planned.

Instead, this most British of assets – the ancestral home of 'Land of Hope and Glory' – was carved up among its main rivals. Only the competition authorities in Brussels stood in the way as a potential obstacle. The music production arm would be taken over by Universal Music (an American offshoot of the financially stretched French conglomerate Vivendi). And the valuable publishing arm – with its rights to all the Beatles' music – looks to be heading for the Japanese house Sony, subject to a European Commission competition inquiry.

Meanwhile, companies in the broader manufacturing and high-tech economy continue to fall like dominoes. The quoted engineering firm Charter International is a depressing example. With a pedigree dating back to the nineteenth century, it was one of those mid-sized engineering groups which form part of the much-lamented supply chain.

The less glamorous arm was engaged in industrial welding and suffered from the global economic slowdown. The more exciting arm, known as Howden, with big operations in Scotland and Northern Ireland, manufactured industrial-scale fans for power stations. This was a growth business, feeding the voracious demand for generation capacity in the emerging markets of Asia as well as Britain. Yet Charter was allowed to vanish into the hands of the smaller US engineering concern Colfax, putting its UK headquarters, future investment and jobs at risk.

Other recent losses have included the sale of software writer Autonomy to America's Hewlett-Packard in 2011 and the sale of the bus and train operator Arriva to Germany's Deutsche Bahn in 2010. Not to mention the sale of Chloride to America's Emerson, the takeover of Tomkins by Canadian concern Onex and the sale of engineering consultants Scott Wilson to American competitor URS in the same year.

Meanwhile, as the new coalition sought to reduce the public debt mountain, an austerity auction began with the £2.1 billion sale of High Speed One, the Channel Tunnel rail link, to a pair of Canadian pension funds. And so the deals went on. In July 2010, Tate & Lyle sold its historic sugars business, including its Golden Syrup factory in London, to American Sugar Refining for £211 million. In October, American private equity group J. C. Flowers took a 40 per cent stake in the Kent Reliance Building Society.

In the same period there have been two reprieves. High-tech sector Micro Focus – which updates ageing computer systems and tests software and which came under siege in the spring of 2011 from private equity firms Advent and Bain Capital – was able to repel the £890 million bid. And around the same time security printer De La Rue, which produces sterling banknotes for the Bank of England, saw off a £925 million hostile bid from French interloper Oberthur. As I commented in the *Daily Mail*: 'It would be hard to be comfortable with the idea that the production of banknotes should be in overseas hands, particularly those of a company with so little disclosure.'

These small victories apart, it's tempting to agree with commentator Will Hutton that 'The "foreign takeovers" horse well and truly has bolted.' But is it within anyone's power to do anything about it?

The answer has to be yes. When the chips are down, it's extraordinary what politicians find they can do. This was apparent – in, admittedly, a less than satisfactory way – when in 2008 Gordon Brown personally assured Sir Victor Blank, Chairman of Lloyds TSB, that the government would not stand in the way if the bank were to take over Halifax Bank of Scotland (HBOS). The deal duly went ahead despite the fact that it ceded Lloyds more than 30 per cent of Britain's huge retail banking market and breached European Commission rules.

This suggests that the problem is one of will rather than capability. A measure of the current government's pusillanimous approach came in 2010–2011 when Rupert Murdoch embarked on his attempt to buy out the minority interest in BSkyB. Vince Cable was outraged, and voiced his concerns in a way that became public. In December 2010 he told *Daily Telegraph* reporters, posing as constituents in his Twickenham constituency: 'I have declared war on Mr Murdoch.' The coalition government as a whole, however, bent over backwards to help Murdoch. It was only when the phone hacking scandal at the *News of the World* became a national issue that the proposed £10 billion takeover imploded.

This seems very much in line with David Cameron's arguments

at the time of the Kraft deal. 'We are an open, global economy. We cannot start creating ownership barriers, trade barriers and protectionist barriers.' And it chimes with the views of then CBI chief Richard Lambert, previously a critic of the foreign takeover free-for-all, who stated that he did not favour any extension of ministerial power, partly because he was worried who would determine 'national interest', partly because he wondered what sort of test would be suitable.

No one who is concerned about the current situation urges a Little England approach that would effectively close off the entire economy. But there is a balance that can be struck – the sort of balance one can find in countries such as Germany where key sectors and infrastructure enjoy a measure of protection. Free market think tank Civitas has, for example, called for measures to be put in place to look at issues of public interest when foreign takeovers are on the cards. Former Cadbury management have called for tougher rules regarding the sale of shares. Former Chairman Roger Carr, battle-hardened by the experience of seeing the company sold from under him, proposed that in future a super-majority of 60 per cent of shareholders should be required to win control of a company.

Some have even suggested a 'Cadbury's Law' that would involve a more thorough vetting process for foreign deals, with the Takeover Panel taking a greater role than previously. In evidence to the Commons Business, Innovation & Skills Committee, Professor Chris Bones of the Henley Business School argued the case for categorising strategic assets to isolate those that could be said to be of national importance. While he voiced his opposition to blanket government intervention he did think conditions could be imposed to protect strategic assets such as skill bases and centres of research and development.

In its findings, the committee said that it was clear that the Companies Act of 2006 had not resolved major issues in corporate governance, such as the role of boards in representing the broader stakeholder interest. The committee argued that in weighing up potential deals, boards invariably feel that their fiduciary duty is to obtain the best price for shareholders, rather than to consider the impact the deal might have on the workforce, suppliers and the broader economy. A detailed inquiry into the role of shareholders and managers of companies was clearly necessary. The committee concluded:

> Recent experience of the behaviour of boards and share-holders in situations ranging from the fall of RBS to the Kraft acquisition of Cadbury indicate that it is time to reconsider many aspects of corporate governance.

The focus shifted to the City's semi-voluntary Takeover Panel, designed to police takeovers in Britain. It was asked to examine whether there was a case for blocking takeovers of strategic assets, deals in which overseas buyers would control 50 per cent of the UK market, and whether deals that would lead to brands moving offshore should be permitted.

The Panel, an instinctively conservative forum cautious about exceeding its relatively narrow mandate, fought shy of some of the more forceful suggestions. Instead it came up with narrower proposals for changing the Takeover Code. These included lifting the '50 per cent plus one' minimum acceptance condition threshold for a takeover and requiring bidders to provide more information in relation to the financing of takeover bids. The former was ultimately rejected, but the requirement that financing terms be disclosed was approved.

There are some who would argue that such a cautious venture goes nowhere near far enough. Hugh Davidson, co-founder of Oxford Strategic Marketing and author of *The Committed Enterprise*, is just one who argues for a shortlist of strategic national assets, featuring such names as Diageo, GlaxoSmithKline, AstraZeneca, Tesco, BP and Vodafone.

Another, more thorough-going approach would be to set up a commission, sitting under the chairmanship of a major industrialist, that would review the implications of the foreign takeover revolution in terms of its impact on the national economy, jobs, research and development and innovation, the tax system and national and energy security. During the period that the commission was in existence, a temporary moratorium would be placed on bids except in the most extenuating circumstances. That would ensure that it reported swiftly (the Independent Commission on Banking, headed by Sir John Vickers – which reported in July 2010 just a year after it was set up – provides a useful model of how effective time limiting can be: it managed to produce the most robust of reforms for the banking system in a fast-changing environment in the financial markets).

Various specific issues would need to be addressed by the commission. First of all, it would have to review the relationship between shareholders and the companies they own. One of the problems with the way takeovers currently operate is that the get-rich-quick elements – the hedge funds, speculators, and private equity princelings – have too great, and often baleful, an influence. Ideally, when a takeover is mooted, only those shareholders that have held stock for six months or more should be allowed to vote and a super majority as high perhaps as 75 per cent (generally required anyway in a scheme of arrangement) should be mandatory before a company can be acquired.

At the same time, a commission might want to consider the case for boards of directors tearing up all existing contracts with director-level executives so that any incentives to sell are invalidated. Arguably, there should be no takeover clauses that require contracts to be paid in full. Only paid-up share options should be honoured, severance deals should be on the same basis as other senior managers in the company (never more than 12 months) and there should be no augmentation of pensions and other arrangements. In other words the board should be judging a takeover bid on the basis of its merits, not on how rich it will make individual directors.

In addition, a commission would need to consider whether directors recommending bids should take into account not just the views of shareholders but of all stakeholders including the workforce, suppliers, consumers and if possible the national interest. Were that to happen, then a two-tier share structure, as in parts of the Continent, might need to be introduced.

Regulatory arrangements would require reviewing. A strong case can be made for expanding the Competition Commission and giving it a much wider remit. All major takeovers, not just those that appear to threaten domestic competition, would need to be examined in the light of their impact not just on markets but on the broader national economic interest.

The Takeover Panel would similarly need to be reviewed. As an informal referee it has been enormously successful, avoiding the protracted and legalistic approach to bids and deals in the US and elsewhere. But any prejudice in favour of bidders needs to be removed. One suggestion is that after initial disclosures 'put up or shut up' timetables should be narrowed. Undertakings made during the course of takeovers – such as promises to keep research and development in the UK or not to close factories – should have the force of the law behind them. Financing details and the plans for repatriation of borrowings should be clearly set out.

The commission would need to examine the world of smaller deals. A case could be made for setting up regional panels to consider such factors as the degree of leverage involved and the likely impact of that on future investment and operations.

And finally, the commission would need to consider the setting up of robust government-controlled institutions – operated on commercial grounds – which could step in to save assets in danger of being sold off on the cheap to foreign buyers.

There might even be a British Investment Bank headed by a senior industrialist. It could have the power to raise funds in the market, rather in the manner of the European Investment Bank and World Bank, to step in and save valuable assets for the nation before selling them on or floating them back on the stock market.

This may sound like a call for heavy-handed state intervention – the sort of intervention that became anathema in the 1970s and 1980s when people could see for themselves how badly government handled corporations like British Leyland. But here government is not being invited to run concerns, only to monitor their position within the British economy, just as German politicans consider the well-being of the country as a whole when looking at foreign bids for German companies. And, of course, government involvement is not automatically a disaster. After all, our most successful industrial group Rolls-Royce aerospace only exists as Britain's biggest exporter because of careful reconstructing under government tutelage.

Half a century ago there was relatively little foreign ownership of corporate and other assets in Britain. In 1963 more than half of the UK stock market was still controlled by individuals, rather than large investment groups, with only 7 per cent in overseas hands.

The mood among established British firms was confident, complacent even. The last thing that they were worried about was being bought by an overseas predator. Much of the action was in the other direction, with ambitious mining finance groups like Rio Tinto and Lonrho buying natural resources assets and the leading auction house Sotheby's enthusiastically buying up its foreign rivals.

Thatcher's revolution transformed the British economic and financial landscape. It lifted the dead hand of the state, encouraged enterprise and self-reliance and allowed the City of London to develop into the most important financial centre in the world – a real rival to New York and Wall Street. But in the process the pendulum swung against British business which, at times, became a plaything for the international speculators.

It is time to redress the balance.

Appendix: Foreign Purchases of UK Firms: A Timeline of Key Deals

1925

Vauxhall Motors sold to General Motors for $2.5 million

General Motors: Detroit-based US car maker with vast US and growing international market.

Vauxhall Motors: Luton-based motor manufacturer of cars and vans established in 1857.

1928

60 per cent of Ford of Britain and European Ford factories bought by Ford Motor Company of USA for £7 million

Ford of Britain: UK car maker began production at Trafford Park in Manchester in 1903.

Ford Motor Company: Founded by Henry Ford in Dearborn, Michigan in 1903. It is the fifth largest car maker in the world.

1951–1960

Ferguson sold to Massey-Harris of Canada for £10 million

Ferguson-Brown: Founded as a tractor maker in 1934 and launched the hydraulic lift for ploughs and other implements.

Massey-Harris: A farm machinery firm founded in Newcastle, Ontario in 1849. After the merger with Ferguson takes the emblematic brand name Massey-Ferguson.

1964

Chrysler Corporation buys one-third control of Rootes. Takes full control in 1967

Chrysler Corporation: Founded in the US by Walter Chrysler in 1925.

Rootes: Brands including Sunbeam, Talbot, Darracq, Hillman, Humber and Singer dated back to 1901. The 1967 sale was done only after exchange controls were exempted and with the agreement of Industrial Re-organisation Corporation which acquired a stake.

1967

Regent Petroleum sold to Texaco of the USA

Regent: In 1947, Texaco Petroleum Products and Trinidad Leasing merge to form the Regent Oil Company selling branded petrol to the UK market.

Texaco: Formed in 1901 as the Texas Oil Company in Beaumont, Texas.

1969

Australian publisher Rupert Murdoch buys *News of the World* for £34 million

Rupert Murdoch: 37-year-old Australian newspaper tycoon beats rival Robert Maxwell in contested takeover.

News of the World: Founded in 1969, Britain's best-selling Sunday newspaper closed its doors in 2011 amid allegations of phone hacking.

November 1976
Observer **sold to Atlantic Richfield for one pound**
Observer: Britain's oldest newspaper founded in 1791. Resold first to Lonrho then Guardian Media Group in 1993.
Atlantic Richfield: Part of Standard Oil founded in 1866. Became a separate exploration company in 1911 and was sold to Britain's BP in 1999.

1984
Al-Fayed brothers take 30 per cent stake in House of Fraser which owns Harrods. Remaining shares purchased in 1985 for £615 million
Harrods: Leading department store in Knightsbridge with international reputation for top quality.
Mohamed Al-Fayed: Egyptian-born businessman based in UK developing portfolio of upmarket brands, such as the 1979 purchase of The Ritz Hotel in Paris.

Early 1988
Rowntree Mackintosh sold to Swiss giant Nestlé for £4.5 billion
Rowntree Mackintosh: Chocolate manufacturer founded in York in 1862, produced famous brands such as KitKat, Aero, Smarties, Rolo and Quality Street.
Nestlé: The product of the 1905 merger between the Anglo-Milk Company and Nestlé which traces its history back to Henri Nestlé in 1866. Controls 6,000 brands and employs 280,000 people worldwide. Well known for its milk formula, condensed milk and Nescafé, the first instant coffee brand.

1990
ICL 80 per cent stake bought by Fujitsu of Japan

ICL: Computer manufacturer, successor to British Tabulating Machines founded in 1907. The company was transformed into ICL as a result of a series of mergers in 1967–1968, becoming the largest computer manufacturer outside the USA. Manufacturer of computer hardware, software and services.

Fujitsu: Founded in 1923 is the leading Japanese information, communications and technology firm. Employs 170,000 people worldwide. Income $55 billion.

Early 1994
Car maker Land Rover sold to Germany's BMW

Land Rover: Control of iconic off-road vehicle Land Rover came as part of BMW's deal to take over Rover Group.

BMW: The luxury car maker had access to Land Rover's unique wheel base technology, but sold brand to Ford for £1.85 billion in 2000, who combined it with Jaguar. Ford sold on to India's Tata Group in March 2008 for £1.1 billion.

May 1995
Merchant bank SG Warburg bought by Swiss Banking Corporation for £856 million

SG Warburg: A ground-breaking London-based merchant bank founded by German-Jewish financier Siegmund Warburg in 1946.

Swiss Banking Corporation: Formed in Basel in 1854 from six smaller banks. Merged in 1998 with Union Bank of Switzerland.

July 1995
Stockbroker Smith New Court sold to Merrill Lynch of the USA for £526 million

Smith New Court: Successor to stockjobbers Smith Brothers in which N. M. Rothschild was a major shareholder.

Merrill Lynch: Founded in New York in 1907 and world's best known stockbroking firm. Sold to Bank of America in 2008 at height of financial crisis.

July 1996
London Electricity sold to America's Entergy for £1.3 billion
London Electricity: Regional electricity company serving the capital and privatised in mid-1980s. Initially featured as management buyout.
Entergy: New Orleans-based power supplier to southern states of the US.

October 1996
France's Connex awarded South Eastern rail franchise
South Eastern: Valuable rail franchise which included the famous London to Brighton line.
Connex: Owned by French conglomerate Vivendi, its franchise was due to last until 2011, but withdrawn in 2003 due to customer unrest and poor management.

November 1997
Mercury Asset Management sold to Merrill Lynch of USA for £3.1 billion
Mercury: Founded in 1969 as fund management arm of bankers SG Warburg. At the time of the takeover it managed assets for more than half of FTSE 100 companies.
Merrill Lynch: New York stockbrokers founded in 1907. Mercury brand was banished by new owners in 2000.

November 1998
Entergy sells London Electricity to France's EDF for £1.9 billion

London Electricity: Regional electricity company serving the capital and privatised in mid–1980s. Initially featured as management buyout.

EDF (Electricité de France): French state-owned electricity supplier bought up business when European power market deregulated.

June 1999

Wal-Mart of the US buys supermarket group Asda for £6.7 million

Wal-Mart: Founded in 1962 by Sam Walton in Rogers, Arkansas it is the world's biggest retailer (branded Walmart since 2008).

Asda: Formed in Leeds in 1949 as Associated Dairies and Farm Stores. It is a pioneer of edge-of-town shopping superstores in the UK.

October 1999

British Steel merges with Dutch rival Hoogovens

British Steel: Company emerged from old nationalised industry of the post-war years with plants throughout Britain and contracts around the world.

Koninklijke Hoogovens: Founded in 1917 and whose business largely catered for home market. Group renamed.

January 2000

America's Citigroup buys Schroders' investment banking arm for £1.36 billion

Citigroup: Founded as City Bank of New York in 1812. Operates in 100 countries and has 200 million clients.

Schroders: Merchant bank moved to London from Hamburg in 1804 and traded as J. F. Schroder and Co.

January 2000
Courtaulds Textiles sold to Sara Lee of USA for £150 million
Courtaulds: Founded in 1794 by George Courtauld and Britain's largest producer of lingerie and underwear employing 20,000 people across 16 countries. Biggest customer is Marks & Spencer in the UK.

Sara Lee: Named after daughter of baker Charles Lubin who sold his business to Chicago-based Consolidated Foods in 1956. Firm changed its name to Sara Lee in 1985. Main products include bakery goods, coffee and processed meat.

April 2000
Robert Fleming & Co sold to Chase Manhattan Bank of New York for $7.7 billion
Robert Fleming & Co: Founded in 1873 as a jute manufacturer in Dundee Scotland, later became a fund manager and City-based investment bank.

Chase Manhattan: Began trading in 1799 as the Manhattan Company, founded by Aaron Burr. Moved from clean water to commercial banking.

May 2000
Mobile phone operator Orange sold to France Telecom for £26.9 billion
Orange: Founded in Britain in April 1994, with the assistance of capital from Hong Kong's Hutchison, it became the UK's number one mobile operator in July 2001.

France Telecom: Semi-privatised telecoms company that is a spin-off from the Ministry of Post and Telegraphs founded in 1878. It has a turnover of €45 billion and employs 180,000 people worldwide.

November 2000

Thames Water sold to Germany's multi-utility RWE for £4.3 billion

Thames Water: Created in 1975 and serving Greater London, the Thames Valley, Surrey, Gloucestershire, Wiltshire, Kent.

RWE: Essen-based group owning companies in Europe and the US, later adding Yorkshire Power to its portfolio.

January 2001

Blue Circle sold to Lafarge of France for £3.1 million

Blue Circle: Founded in 1900 from the merger of UK regional cement companies.

Lafarge: Dates back to 1833 as a limestone producer in the Ardeche. Products include cement, gypsum and other construction materials.

March 2002

Energy supplier npower (formerly Innogy) sold to RWE for £3 billion

npower: Formed out of the old National Power company, it was the UK's third largest supplier of gas and electricity with 6 million customers.

RWE: Essen-based group owning companies in Europe and the US, later adding Yorkshire Power to its portfolio.

June 2003

Chelsea FC sold to Russian Roman Abramovich for £140 million

Chelsea FC: Hugely in debt until the 2003 rescue, since when the £740 million pumped in has brought success and turned them into one of football's leading clubs.

Roman Abramovich: Russian oligarch, now London-based, with estimated fortune of £11 billion arising from minerals and energy deals after the break-up of the Soviet Union.

Late 2003

Retailer Debenhams sold to two US-based private equity firms CVC Capital Partners and Texas Pacific

Debenhams: Trading since 1813, it has flagship department store in London with around 160 branches throughout the UK, Ireland and Denmark and franchise stores in other countries.

CVC Capital and Texas Pacific: American-founded but operating around the world, they are among the leading private equity firms devoting funds largely to management buyouts.

Early 2004

Amersham sold to America's GE Healthcare for £9 billion

Amersham: Pharmaceuticals firm specialising in medical diagnostics and life science products. Its roots were in the post-war development and manufacture of radioactive materials for uses in medicine, scientific research and industry.

GE Healthcare: US company employing more than 46,000 people worldwide but with headquarters in Buckinghamshire.

September 2004

Southern Cross Healthcare sold to US private equity firm Blackstone for £162 million

Southern Cross: Fourth largest provider in the UK residential and nursing long-term care market for both the elderly and enduring mental health patients. Operating 160 care homes with approximately 8,200 beds. Later the same year buys BHP which has a securitised property portfolio and Highfield Care which operates a further 192 homes.

Blackstone: Leading private equity firm with major deals, such as Universal Studios and Madame Tussauds, to its name. By 2011, $157 billion of assets under management.

Autumn 2004
Abbey bank sold to Spain's Santander for £8.6 billion
Abbey: A building society dating from 1836, it grew through mergers to gain a modern reputation for innovation. Converted to a bank in 1989 with its shares peaking in 2000.
Santander Group: Madrid-based, it operates mainly in Western Europe, Latin America and the US. One of the largest banks in the world in terms of market capitalisation.

May 2005
Manchester United sold to America's Glazer family for £800 million
Manchester United: Most famous football club in England, whose huge success in domestic and European competitions created a global brand.
Glazers: Led by Malcolm Glazer, Florida-based owners of franchised sports teams in US purchased in highly leveraged deals.

July 2005
Remnants of car maker MG Rover sold to China's Nanjing Automobile
MG Rover: Last mass market motor group was formed when BMW sold the car-making and engine manufacturing assets of the original Rover Group to the Phoenix Consortium for £10 in 2000. It went into administration in 2005.
Nanjing Automobile Corp: State-owned operation dating back to

1947, making it China's oldest vehicle producer. It manufactures cars, trucks and buses.

August 2005
British Plaster Board sold to France's Saint-Gobain for £3.9 billion

British Plaster Board: Founded in 1916 and at the time it was sold the world's largest manufacturer of plaster boards.

Saint-Gobain: Diversified construction products firm with a history dating back to 1665.

October 2005
Mobile phone operator MmO2 was taken over by Telefonica of Spain for £18 billion

MmO2: The mobile arm of BT which was floated as a separate company in 2001. Has 40 million customers across Europe.

Telefonica: Founded in 1924, Spain's monopoly telecoms group was spun off and opened to competition in 1997. It has an extensive business in Latin America.

February 2006
Westinghouse sold to Japan's Toshiba for $5.4 billion

Westinghouse Corporation: The world leader in power station construction, an arm of state-owned British Nuclear Fuels Limited (BNFL).

Toshiba Corporation: Formed in 1939, with headquarters in Tokyo, the multinational company specialises in electronics, electrical equipment and information technology.

March 2006
Shipping group P&O sold to Dubai Ports World for $6.8 billion

P&O (Peninsular and Oriental Steam Navigation Company):
Founded in 1830s with an unparalleled international infrastructure of container ports and ships.
Dubai Ports World: United Arab Emirates state-owned company
handling marine ports worldwide with 49 terminals in operation
and more under development.

June 2006
**British Airports Authority (BAA) sold to Spain's Ferrovial group
for £10.6 billion**
BAA: Owned and operated airports that handled 63 per cent of
travellers going in and out of the country. As well as London's
Heathrow, Gatwick and Stansted, it ran regional airports such as
Glasgow, Edinburgh, Birmingham, Manchester and Southampton.
Ferrovial: Madrid-based family-controlled Spanish construction
group with projects worldwide, notably the 1992 Barcelona Olympics.

June 2006
Glass maker Pilkington sold to Nippon Sheet Glass for £1.8 billion
Pilkington: Founded in 1826 in St Helens, Lancashire, a global
pioneer in modern, float glass production. It employs almost
24,000 people and, along with St Helens, has factories in
Birmingham and Doncaster.
Nippon Sheet Glass: Formed in 1916 through an American
collaboration, it expanded throughout Japan after 1945. Based in
Tokyo.

July 2006
**Associated British Ports (ABP) sold to foreign consortium for
£3.17 billion**
ABP: Originally the British Transport Docks Board, it became the

largest UK ports operator handling a quarter of UK's seaborne trade from 21 domestic facilities.

September 2006
British Oxygen sold to Germany's Linde for £8.2 billion
British Oxygen (BOC) Group: Multinational industrial gas company with over 30,000 employees on six continents and sales of over £4.6 billion.
Linde Group: Munich-based international industrial gases and engineering company founded in 1879.

November 2006
Energy firm Scottish Power sold to Spain's Iberdrola for £12 billion
Scottish Power: Glasgow-based energy supplier operating in central and southern Scotland and the Merseyside and North Wales regions.
Iberdrola: Bilbao-based private utility, it has around 33,000 employees in over 40 countries on four continents serving around 30 million customers.

December 2006
Tobacco firm Gallaher sold to Japan Tobacco for £7.5 billion
Gallaher: Tobacco firm founded in Derry in Northern Ireland in 1857. The key brands include Benson & Hedges, Silk Cut and Hamlet Cigars.
Japan Tobacco: Formed in 1985. Domestic tobacco brands, foods and pharmaceuticals.

January 2007
Alliance-Boots sold to foreign consortium for £12 billion

Alliance-Boots: Chain chemists Boots, an iconic business on Britain's high streets, merged with Alliance Unichem in July 2006.
Stefano Pessina: Italian pharmacy giant.
KKR: New York private equity firm.

January 2007
Steelmaker Corus sold to India's Tata for £6.2 billion
Corus: The Anglo-Dutch company was formed in 1999 from the old British Steel operation with plants throughout Britain. Sixth largest steelmaker in world.
Tata: Multinational conglomerate based in interests in communications, IT, engineering, materials, services, energy, consumer products and chemicals. The Group has operations in more than 80 countries.

February 2007
Liverpool FC sold to US consortium for £285 million
Liverpool FC: Previously highly successful club domestically and in Europe which became a global brand.
Tom Hicks and George Gillett: Took over with borrowings with further debt added which hampered the club's fortunes. Resold in 2010, to another American, John W. Henry, whose New England Sports Ventures bought it for £300 million.

August 2007
ICI sold to Dutch firm AkzoNobel for £8 billion
ICI (Imperial Chemical Industries): Iconic and innovative group whose wide range of products, from paint and chemicals to synthetic materials, were famous the world over. Spin-off companies developed such as AstraZeneca, Syngenta and Victrex.

AkzoNobel: Conglomerate selling decorative paints, performance coatings and speciality chemicals. Based in Amsterdam, the company trades in more than 80 countries with a workforce of over 55,000 people.

January 2008
Scottish & Newcastle sold to Heineken and Carlsberg for £7.6 million

Scottish & Newcastle: Britain's last domestically owned mass-market beer producer with a history of brewing distinctive beer, including Newcastle Brown, dating back to 1749. It had been highly successful in breaking into the fast-growing Russian beer market.

Carlsberg and Heineken: Danish and Dutch family-controlled brewing giants seeking to dominate the UK market place and gain full control of S & N's Russian brewing partnerships.

Early 2008
Burren Energy sold to Italy's ENI for £1.7 billion

Burren Energy: Formed in 1994, it developed its business in Turkmenistan and West Africa leading to a 2003 flotation with a market capitalisation of £175 million.

ENI: One-third owned by the state, the multinational oil and gas company operates in 70 countries and is Italy's largest industrial company.

August 2008
Manchester City sold to Abu Dhabi group

Manchester City: Largely unsuccessful football club, but with a new stadium and Premier League status the club attracted Thai investor who later sold on.

ADUG led by Sheikh Mansour: Mansour is one of the world's wealthiest individuals, who has sunk £750 million into the club, making it among the world's top 20.

Late 2008 and early 2009
British Energy sold to EDF for £12.5 billion
British Energy: The nation's largest electricity generator operated eight former UK state-owned nuclear power stations and one coal-fired power station.
EDF: French state-owned energy supplier.

July 2009
Engineers Tomkins sold to Canadian consortium for £2.9 billion
Tomkins: Global company, its largest division is Industrial & Automotive, trading primarily under Dexter Axle, Gates, Ideal Clamp Products and Schrader Electronics.
Onex Corporation: Toronto-based private equity firm investing in a wide array of industries where it drives down costs.
Canada Pension Plan Investment Board: Created in 1997, by June 2011 it had $153.2 billion in assets under management.

October 2009
Lufthansa takes full control of Bmi by buying a 20 per cent stake from SAS for £38 million
Bmi: Founded in 1949 as Derby Aviation and developed into the regional carrier British Midland by Sir Michael Bishop who sold his 50 per cent stake to Lufthansa for £223 million in early 2009.
Lufthansa: Began operations in the 1920s as German flag carrier used largely by politicians. Now among Europe's largest carriers. Bmi sold to British Airways in 2012.

January 2010
Cadbury sold to America's Kraft Foods for £11.5 billion
Kraft Foods: American-owned multinational with famous brands Kraft Cheese Slices, Maxwell House coffee, Philadelphia cream cheese, Ritz and Danone crackers. By 2009 employed 98,000 people in 168 plants with annual sales of over £26 billion.

Cadbury: Bournville-based and originally family owned chocolate makers with worldwide brands such as Dairy Milk, Wispa, Crunchie and Curly Wurly. Workforce of around 40,000 operating in 60 countries.

March 2010
UK Lottery operator Camelot sold to Ontario Teachers' Pension Fund for £389 million
Camelot Group: Owned by a British consortium including Cadbury Schweppes, De La Rue, ICL and Racal which was awarded the first National Lottery licence in 1993 and retained it ever since. It has raised £24 billion for good causes.

Ontario Teachers' Pension Fund: Big Canadian public sector investor (equivalent of a sovereign wealth fund) that owns Bristol and Birmingham airports and 27 per cent of Northumberland Water.

April 2010
Transport firm Arriva sold to Deutsche Bahn for £1.5 billion
Arriva: Northern-based group started in Sunderland in 1920s. Rail franchise operator and runner of many of the Britain's big city bus networks. Expanded successfully into the Netherlands, Germany and other markets.

Deutsche Bahn: Partly state-owned rail operator begun in 1994 to succeed the East and West German national railways. It carries 2 billion passengers a year.

August 2010

International Power merges with French giant

International Power: International electricity generator formed in 2000 by the demerger of National Power. Specialised in bringing modern generation plants and advice to developing countries.

GDF SUEZ: French multinational energy company operating in electricity generation and distribution, natural gas and renewable energy.

March 2011

Forth Ports sold to foreign consortium for £754 million

Forth Ports: Runs the historic Tilbury Docks in London together with 400 acres of Edinburgh waterfront and four ports around the Scottish coast.

Takeover Consortium: Led by Germany's Deutsche Bank and including several European investors.

August 2011

Software group Autonomy sold to US's Hewlett-Packard for £7.1 billion

Autonomy: Founded in 1996 and based in the Silicon Fen high-tech park, the company is a market leader using technologies arising from Cambridge University research.

Hewlett-Packard: California-based IT corporation operating around the world in IT products, technologies, software services to businesses and individual consumers.

September 2011

Charter International sold to Colfax of USA for £1.5 billion

Charter: Founded by Royal Charter in 1889 as the British South-

Africa Company. It is now an engineering company specialising in welding and industrial cooling equipment.

Colfax: Industrial holding company formed in 1995 involved in fluid handling and mechanical power chains.

January 2012

Dairy firm Robert Wiseman sold to German conglomerate Müller for £280 million

Robert Wiseman: Founded in 1949 and floated in 1994, the company accounts for one-third of all milk sold in UK.

Müller: Began as small Bavarian dairy by Ludwig Müller, the yoghurt and dessert giant buys 219 billion litres of milk a year in the UK.

January 2012

8.68 per cent stake in Thames Water sold to China Investment Corporation for £500 million

Thames Water: Traces its origins back to the New River Company founded in 1600. Now under the majority control of Australia infrastructure group Macquarie.

CIC: Founded in 2002 by the People's Republic of China to invest Beijing's financial surpluses overseas.

Select Bibliography

Brummer, Alex and Cowe, Roger, *Weinstock* (London: HarperCollins Business 1998)

Brummer, Alex, *The Crunch* (London: Random House Business Books 2009)

Business, Innovation and Skills Committee, *Mergers, acquisitions and takeovers: the takeover of Cadbury by Kraft* (House of Commons Ninth Report of Session 2009–10)

Cable, Vince, *Speech to All Party Parliamentary Corporate Governance Group* (4 April 2011)

Cadbury, Deborah, *Chocolate Wars* (London: HarperPress 2010)

Carr, Roger, *Speech Said Business School* (9 February 2010)

Cartwright, Susan, 'Why Mergers Fail and How to Prevent It.' In *Business: the ultimate resource* (Editors of Perseus Publishing 2002)

Cummings, Chris, *Key Facts about UK Financial and Professional Services* (The City UK September 2011)

Darling, Alistair, *Back from the Brink* (London: Atlantic Books 2011)

Davis, Evan, *Made in Britain* (London: Little, Brown 2011)

Ferguson, Niall, *The Ascent of Money* (London: Allen Lane 2008)

Friedman, Thomas, *The World is Flat* (London: Allen Lane 2005)

Froud, Julie et al., *KNOWING WHAT TO DO? How not to build trains* (Manchester: CRESC Research Report July 2011)

Lawson, Nigel, *The View from No 11* (London: Bantam Press 1992)

Meloria Meschi, *Analytical Perspectives on Mergers and Acquisitions. A survey* (Centre for International Business Studies, South Bank University Paper Number 5–97)

ONS, *Mergers & acquisitions involving UK companies 2nd quarter 2011* (Statistical Bulletin 6 September 2011)

PricewaterhouseCoopers, *The Future of UK Manufacturing* (PWC April 2009)

Skidelsky, Robert et al., *Blueprint for a British Investment Bank* (Centre for Global Studies 2011)

Takeover Panel Code Committee, *Review of Certain Aspects of the Regulation of Takeover Bids* (London: 21 October 2010)

The City UK, Key Facts about UK Financial and Professional Services

Vaitilingam, Romesh, *Research for our Future* (Research Councils UK 2010)

Wilson John F., *British Business History 1720–1994* (Manchester: Manchester University Press 1995)

Index